KITCHENS AND BATHROOMS

Make It Right®

KITCHENS AND BATHROOMS

MIKE HOLMES

Collins

Make It Right ®
Kitchens and Bathrooms
Text copyright © 2010 Restovate Ltd. All rights reserved.

Published by Collins, an imprint of HarperCollins Publishers Ltd

First Canadian edition

HarperCollins books may be purchased for educational, business, or sales promotional use through our Special Markets Department.

HarperCollins Publishers Ltd
2 Bloor Street East, 20th Floor
Toronto, Ontario, Canada
M4W 1A8

www.harpercollins.ca

Library and Archives Canada Cataloguing in Publication

Holmes, Mike
Make it right : kitchens and bathrooms / Mike Holmes.

ISBN 978-1-55468-033-7

1. Kitchens—Remodeling. 2. Bathrooms—Remodeling.
I. Title. II. Title: Kitchens and bathrooms.
TH4816.3.K58H63 2009   643'.3   C2009-903152-3

Printed and bound in Canada
TC 9 8 7 6 5 4 3 2 1

Photography Credits:
123 Bamboo, p. 144; American Standard, pp. 168, 171, 174, 176; Bianca Auciello, p. 109; BASF, p. 45; Mark Bernardi, pp. 80, 84, 150; Blanco, pp. 117, 118; Blum Canada, 108; Caesarstone, p. 128; Dreamstime, p. 71; Forbo, p. 139; Holmes Group, pp. 13, 16, 23, 26, 30, 52, 74, 190; Home Depot, pp. 134, 141; iStock photo, pp. 4, 8, 11, 20, 60, 62, 67, 86, 92, 96, 125, 126, 154, 156, 158; Jeld-Wen, pp. 47, 48, 50; Barbara Kamienski, pp. 33, 36; Kohler, pp. 64, 104, 120, 121, 122, 159, 163, 169, 172; Kraftmaid, pp. 95, 106, 107; Joseph Marranca, pp. xii, 18, 22, 32, 37, 39, 56, 153, 173; M. Teixeira Soapstone, p. 127; NuHeat, p. 38; Quality Craft, pp. 136, 137, 184; Second Wind Timber, p. 89; Solatube, pp. 53,164; Tilemaster/Holton Impex International, p. 183.

To the next generation of skilled trades workers—
you will continue to make it right.

CONTENTS

KITCHENS AND BATHROOMS

INTRODUCTION

A homeowner recently told me about his new kitchen cabinets. They stink. They're off-gassing like crazy. He can't live in his condo because everyone notices the smell—except, of course, the company that supplied the cabinets—and now he has to replace them. In hindsight, he wishes he'd chosen low-VOC cabinets that don't off-gas as much, but he didn't know at the time that they were an option.

It's too bad, because not many renovation projects can give you as much satisfaction as a new kitchen or bathroom. But I'm willing to bet no other renovation project will bring up more choices than a kitchen or bathroom. What do you do first? How do you find the best people to work for you? What about tile, countertops, cabinetry, flooring, appliances? The list goes on and on.

The fact is lots of choices can be good choices. There isn't one right answer that works for everyone, because people have different budgets, different needs, different ideas, different things they're looking for. What matters is figuring out what's important to you and why. Are you looking for the best quality? The lowest cost? The kind of products that will last a lifetime? And what about the environmental impact?

Maybe you feel overwhelmed by how much there is to know. Believe me, I'm still learning all the time too. There are new products and materials on the market every day, and new techniques and tools being introduced, and it can be a lot of work to stay on top of it all.

In the pages that follow, I'll explain why the real part of any renovation happens behind the walls, and tell you what you need to know about that world behind the walls, including the structure, the plumbing, and the electrical. You might not have thought much about these things yet, but believe me, they're important and they have to be done right if you want to spend your money right. You have to look at your kitchen or bathroom as if it's just a small part of a whole system that works together. To do a kitchen or bathroom right, you have to understand the system, you have to understand your whole house and how it works. I spend a lot of time in this book leading you through all the different components that make up your house because they will have a direct effect on how successful your kitchen or bathroom renovation is going to be. So many bad renos happen because the homeowners and the contractors don't want to spend the time or the effort making things right behind the walls first—they just want to jump right into choosing counters and faucets and fancy finishes. That's putting the cart before the horse.

I'm going to take you through the stages of the renovation process, letting you in on some of what I've learned in nearly 30 years in this business. That's what good contractors do: They grab the homeowner and say, "Hey, here's what you need to know. Here's what you need to do to make it right." I'll also tell you how to hire the right contractor, and to do a truly "green" renovation.

Renovating doesn't have to be a nightmare. When you've got the facts and you know what to expect, there's no reason you can't end up with a great reno that adds real value to your home. When it seems like there are too many details, and too much to know, remember that you can always go back to the basics: Slow down. Educate yourself. Check out your contractor. Make smarter choices.

CHAPTER 1

Getting Started

Most homeowners start a renovation by looking at pictures of totally finished rooms—showrooms, really. That's what I call "eye candy." This can be a good way to get ideas, but to be honest, that's not what renovations are all about. *A good renovation is about what's under the surface and behind the walls.* That's my world.

I've often found that homeowners don't notice there's something wrong with their renovation unless the finishes look bad. It's true that bad finishes are a sign that something is wrong, but it usually goes a lot deeper than the surface. Bad finishes—like sloppy trim, cracking grout, or cabinet doors that don't shut properly—are signs of bad workmanship, not enough effort, or just plain ignorance on the part of the contractor or subcontractors. You can bet on one thing: if the finish is bad, the start was probably wrong too.

That's why it's important to take the time to understand your house better. To see that it's not just the finish—the lipstick and mascara—that matters, it's everything that's underneath and behind the finish as well. A house has to be built from the outside in, not from the inside out. You might find it hard to believe, but a successful kitchen or bathroom renovation has more to do with carpentry, HVAC (heating, ventilation, and air conditioning), electrical, and plumbing than tile or paint colours.

So, before we move on to questions like what kind of countertop you should put in the kitchen, we need to look at the bigger picture. You need to understand what this renovation project is going to involve.

Let's start with the questions that most homeowners start with—how much it's going to cost, and how to get more usable space in your kitchen or bathroom without having to add on. In the next chapter, I'll go behind the walls—your house's existing structure, plumbing and drainage, electrical, HVAC, insulation, and windows. You need to get the facts on all of these things if you're going to do the job right.

Money, money, money: How much can you spend?

Your budget is totally up to you. It's based on your income and how much you've saved or how much a bank will lend you—and how much you're comfortable borrowing. How long do you plan to stay in your house? If you plan to grow old in it and you're still young, you might want to spend more than if you plan to move in a few years. You should also factor in the value of housing in your neighbourhood, and figure out whether your investment will "over-improve" the house—that is, make it worth more than any other house in your area. That can be a bad idea, especially if your plan is to get most of your investment back (or even make a profit) by selling within just a few years.

Your budget will also be based on how much that kitchen or bath of your dreams is going to cost. But how do you know how much it will cost? Lots of contractors will be able to give you a ballpark number for your renovation plans. It's not the same thing as a quote, but it could help you figure out if you're being realistic or just dreaming. And keep in mind that if a ballpark estimate is off, it's probably an underestimate rather than an overestimate, so it's a good idea to add at least 10% to any projected budget. That way, you'll be covered if any surprises come up—or if you change your mind along the way and decide to add a few upgrades. Remember: The less you change your mind during the renovation process, the better chance you have of staying on budget and on time. Plan ahead!

Using the services of professionals like designers, architects, and engineers will also add to the cost, and that may not be something you're entirely familiar with at the beginning. By the time you get to the contract stage, you should have a firm number that everybody agrees on, not a hazy "more or less" figure. The only way to get to that firm number is to plan all the details of the reno, including the materials you want, so that your contractor can do exact calculations.

If that first ballpark figure from a contractor comes as a shock, consider your options. You could wait another year or two and continue saving towards your goal. You could make some concessions in your plans to cut costs (going with stock cabinetry rather than custom, for example, or getting mid-range appliances rather than top-of-the-line). Your contractor might have some ideas to help you save or about

how to do the reno in stages. Maybe the major stuff gets started this year, but isn't complete until next year.

You could also borrow more money than you'd planned, but keep in mind that there's always a cost to borrowing money, and the longer it takes to pay off the principal, the more you'll spend on interest. Interest rates have been low for years now, which has made borrowing pretty cheap, but rates could jump at any time, which would increase your payments a whole lot. Those interest rate hikes would affect not only your home improvement loan, but also any other loans you have, such as a car loan and maybe even your mortgage. The extra costs to service your debt could get really big, really fast.

Maybe you're thinking, "Hey, this guy's a contractor, not a financial planner, so why is he giving me advice about money?" The answer is that I want you to be realistic about money so you can be responsible to the people you hire. I'm always standing up for homeowners who've been taken advantage of by lousy contractors, but the flip side is the homeowner who takes advantage of a contractor by not having the money to pay when the work is done. Don't be that kind of homeowner. Be realistic about what your reno will cost so that you can hold up your end of the bargain.

What you can expect to spend when you're renovating a kitchen

The sky's the limit when it comes to some people's kitchen renovations. I've seen renos that cost over $100,000 and nice renos for much less. The quality of the existing plumbing, electrical, and structure will have an impact on the total cost, but the biggest factor has to do with the choices you make. Laminate counters or granite?

I like the look of this range hood too. The size is good. It's useless, though, if it's not vented outside. You also want an 8" vent, minimum.

You see lots of cupboards. I see a lot of display space but very little storage for a big kitchen, and not much counterspace either.

Many homeowners like the look of hardwood, but wood floors aren't the best choice for kitchens or other potentially wet areas.

Standard range hood or designer? Vinyl floor, ceramic, or natural stone? Stock cabinets or custom?

What you can predict fairly accurately is what proportion each part of the renovation should cost. In the following list, you'll see how the costs break down, based on North American averages:

- **Cabinets: 48%**
- **Labour/installation: 16%**
- **Countertops: 13%**
- **Appliances: 8%**
- **Flooring: 4%**
- **Sinks and faucets: 4%**
- **Miscellaneous: 7%**

Source: National Kitchen and Bath Association.

These figures can give you some idea of how to budget. Even if you go with a bare-bones renovation starting at about $15,000, you can expect to pay about half of that on cabinets. As you continue to plan your reno, don't skimp on the stuff you don't see. Expensive tiles are crap if they're not installed correctly on the right subfloor.

What you can expect to spend when you're renovating a bathroom

With bathrooms, you're going to find that labour makes up a big part of the total cost—probably about half. You won't have as much cabinetry as in the kitchen—where cabinets can cost close to 50% of the total—so even if you go custom those cabinets aren't going to account for so much of the cost. If you change the layout of your bathroom fixtures, or add more fixtures (such as a separate shower or a bidet), that's going to cost you more in labour because it's going to take your plumber and carpenter more time than if you'd kept everything in the same place. Once your walls and floors are opened up, you probably want to take the opportunity to upgrade your plumbing, especially if the existing plumbing is on its last legs and could eventually damage your new renovation.

Just like with kitchens, if you want high-end fixtures and products, that's going to cost more. Do you want marble counters on custom cabinets? A separate bathtub and shower, with tempered-glass doors custom-fitted for the shower? Two sinks plus dual-flush toilet and bidet? Tumbled marble tile throughout the bathroom? All that is obviously going to cost a whole lot more than standard fixtures and lower-end tile. An easy rule of thumb is to take the cost of your fixtures and accessories, then add that amount again for labour. That will give you an approximate cost for the whole thing.

Space: How much do you have—and can you find more?

The decision to renovate a kitchen or bathroom is often made because you're frustrated by not having enough space. Not enough space for two people to work in the kitchen or get ready in the morning, not enough space for storage—you know what I'm talking about.

Sometimes issues of space can be dealt with through better organization of what you already have, and that can be the best and least expensive option. But if that's not

possible, you need to look at how a new design can solve those everyday frustrations. A better layout of fixtures, appliances, cabinets, and even passageways to and from the room could be the solution.

When planning your renovation, pay attention to traffic flow. If your kitchen is the entranceway to another room, you don't want an open refrigerator door to get in the way.

To get that new-and-improved layout, it's worth looking at whether there's any floor space in nearby rooms that could be "stolen" and used as part of the

MIKE'S TIP

Before you plan to take down a wall to get more space for your kitchen or bathroom, you have to be sure the wall is *not* supporting the structure of the house! Structural support is also an issue if you're planning to move or enlarge a doorway, move or enlarge a window, or move or add a bathtub. A contractor may have an opinion (even a really good one) about whether the wall is structural, but it will require a structural engineer to actually stamp (approve) the change. Even if you find out that it's safe to take down a wall, be aware that any changes that affect structure can be made only after you submit a permit application (with a plan drawing) to your local building department, and receive a building permit.

Even if the wall is safe to take down, some older houses may have walls with asbestos or mould which are serious health hazards. Pros should weigh in and determine if extra precautions or demolition measures are necessary.

kitchen or bathroom. For example, if there's a bedroom next to the bathroom, does it have any space to spare? Sometimes a bedroom closet can be closed off and easily incorporated into a room on the other side of the wall. This can work if the bedroom is large enough that it already has enough alternative storage space, or more could be built.

Other places you can look for extra space are under stairs (for storage, especially) and in hallways. Sometimes a hallway that's bounded by walls on both sides can be opened up and made into part of a kitchen. By doing this, you might get enough room for an informal eating area, cabinetry for storing small appliances or dishes you hardly ever use, or a larger island.

Just remember that a hallway determines how traffic flows through your house, and if you incorporate an existing hallway into your design, you'll still need to allow that traffic to pass through or find a way to redirect the traffic route. In fact, traffic routes should be part of your overall design strategy. Sometimes it makes sense to move or eliminate a doorway, for instance, to achieve a more efficient flow.

I've seen a lot of houses where homeowners have taken over an entire bedroom to create a larger bathroom, or maybe to add a master bathroom to their floor plan. No doubt about it: a master bath is a big selling feature these days, and it could add value to your house if you put one in. But never do this if you only have three bedrooms to start with. Most realtors will tell you that turning a three-bedroom house into a two-bedroom (even with an ensuite bath) is going to make your house tougher to sell when the time comes. And bedrooms in the basement don't count—only above-ground bedrooms have real value as selling features.

Bay windows are a good way to add more space and natural light. Installing one has to be done right, with permits, because you're affecting the structure of your house.

You might also be thinking about turning a single-family home into a duplex, which will mean at least one more kitchen, and probably another bathroom. Getting some income out of your home is a great idea, but be aware that there are costs involved in making the transition and it may not even be allowed. There are lots of laws and bylaws that you have to follow to make a legal duplex or multiple-unit home. There might also be consequences for your financing, insurance, and even the property taxes you pay. So even though a rental unit might be a good idea, just be realistic about how complicated it really will be to make it happen, and educate yourself. Start by going down to your local city hall, or the building and planning department of your municipality, and making some enquiries. Your city might also have a lot of its regulations listed on its website.

My gut feeling about renos

Gutting a room is usually necessary for a major reno, unless you're working with an almost new house.

You may be thinking, "Won't that be more disruptive than just putting in some new cabinets and fixtures?" Yes, it will, but it's also the most logical thing to do, and the best use of your money. Let me explain why.

Let's say your kitchen has aluminum wiring from the 1970s, 40-year-old galvanized plumbing, and poor insulation. Maybe you don't think there are any problems with the mechanicals right now, but it may be only a question of time before those galvanized pipes corrode and burst, maybe on some cold winter night. And you're probably not aware how much you're paying to heat or cool that room, with all that air escaping through uninsulated walls. Wouldn't it make sense to take those walls apart and get your mechanicals and insulation done right?

To decide if you need to gut the room before updating it, ask yourself these important questions:

What kind of plumbing is in place, and how old is it?

If it's galvanized rather than copper, you need to upgrade to copper or to a newer flexible tubing system such as PEX. If it's a combination of galvanized and copper, you'd be better off replacing the galvanized sections—which are probably in the least-accessible areas. In both cases, taking the walls apart to get at the plumbing is the way to go.

What kind of electrical wiring is in place, and how old is it?

If you have knob-and-tube or aluminum systems, or a combination of either and newer wiring, you should expose the wiring and replace it properly. Most insurers will not insure homes with knob-and-tube, and there is a risk of fire.

Are you hoping to add recessed lighting in the ceiling, or wiring for computers or audio-visual components?

These installations are most easily done with exposed ceiling and walls.

What kind of insulation, if any, is in the walls?

Many older homes were built with little or no insulation, or maybe just some old newspapers stuffed into the walls. That means there's a lot of money and energy being wasted. The quality of insulation materials has grown incredibly in the last couple of decades. With exposed walls, you'll be able to apply the highest-quality insulation (a closed-cell polyurethane foam) and achieve cost savings in your heating and cooling bills for years to come. Ideally, plumbing and HVAC should not be run on exterior walls. But if they're already there and they're not being moved in your reno, they need to be adequately protected from the cold, so insulation is a must.

Is your method of heating and cooling able to handle the changes you want?

If you are planning an extension to your house or thinking of finishing a basement, an HVAC specialist should have a look at your furnace and air conditioner. They may not be big enough. If you are changing the layout of an existing space, HVAC runs and returns may need to be moved.

Are the walls made of plaster and lath?

Plaster-and-lath walls date back to the 1950s at least—and usually a lot earlier—which means that those walls are probably dry and brittle now. They aren't likely to stand up to the beating they'll take during a renovation, and your contractor will spend time (and your money) trying to save them. Why bother? If you're concerned about the waste involved, keep in mind that both plaster and lath are fully recyclable.

Are the tiles in your bathroom cracked, or can you see any other signs that water has penetrated behind the tiles?

If so, you definitely need to take those tiles down and take the wallboard off. Get down to the studs and subfloor to make sure you've taken care of any possible water damage, mould, or rotting wood. You'll also want to determine if the tiles cracked from settling of the house (now long finished) or more recent structural issues.

Keep in mind as well that the various trades who work on your house will be able to work faster and better—ultimately, at less cost to you for their time—if the walls are exposed. You can update all your systems at once, which is cheaper in the long run than trying to do it one at a time. Yes, there's the added cost of new drywall, but the quality of your renovation will increase exponentially if you're willing to go the distance and take the walls back to the studs.

Don't be overwhelmed by the idea that your kitchen or bathroom will be gutted before it's put back together again. Instead, think of the advantages you'll have: more freedom to design, easier access for the people doing the work, and most of all, knowing that your kitchen or bathroom has been done right.

Energy audits are good for the environment and for your bottom line

Once you're serious about starting a major renovation project, you should make an energy audit part of your planning from the very beginning. On top of identifying how you can save energy and money, an audit may make you eligible for government grants. An audit may even help you sell your house down the road. In fact, in some cities and provinces, you will be required to have an energy audit before you sell. It's worth your investment.

There are two phases to every energy audit. Phase one establishes a baseline, or starting point, for your home. You arrange for a certified energy adviser to visit your home and run a series of tests to determine how efficient it is. The adviser will send you a full report, with a set of recommendations for the best retrofit strategies—ranging from increased insulation to replacement of windows, furnace, and water heater, for example—to make your home more efficient.

In phase two of the energy audit, the energy adviser will make a return visit, run some of the same tests, and check to see what you've done to the home. If you're applying for a government grant, the adviser will send this second report to the government for them to write you a cheque.

Permits

Too many people don't think about permits when planning a renovation. They think that permits are just another pain in the butt. They're not. Getting a permit is not just getting a piece of paper so you can stick it in your window. You're actually getting an inspector to ensure that your renovation will be done at least to minimum code so it's not going to burn, fall down, or be unsafe. For me, minimum code is not enough, but it's still important. If the electrical is wrong—like the the time I found 45 junction points in one basement alone—it can be dangerous. Forty-five—I was staggered by this. My electrician was too. The homeowners didn't get a permit and didn't get an inspection.

If you move electrical, you need an electrical permit. If you move plumbing, you need a plumbing permit. If you move a wall, you need a structural permit. If you're just doing a bathroom replacement of the tub, toilet, and sink, you don't need any permits. But if you're adding a new plug or light you need a permit.

Permits are your responsibility. Don't just let your contractor oversee this process. You have to tell them, I want to be there for the inspections. Because if you're

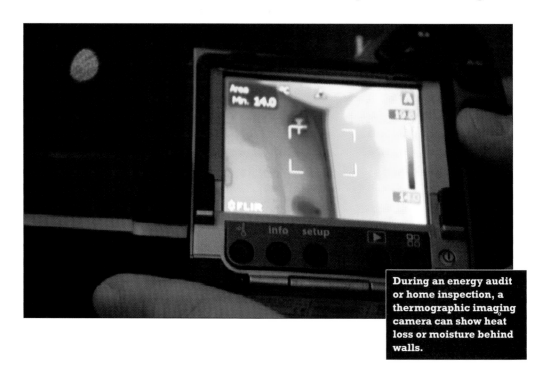

During an energy audit or home inspection, a thermographic imaging camera can show heat loss or moisture behind walls.

there to see what the inspectors have to say about the job then you're part of it. You need to be part of the job. And if a contractor tells you that you don't need a permit and then you do, you are dealing with the wrong contractor. Get rid of them.

A lot of people will avoid getting a permit simply because they think it's going to raise the taxes on their home. Well, it might. But that's a small price to pay compared to what it could cost you to fix it down the road if your reno is not done right.

Slow down

A few years ago, a homeowner asked me about two bathrooms she was trying to have renovated in a hurry for the holidays. She had called a number of contractors and all of them quoted over $80,000 for two bathrooms. She was flabbergasted and asked me if it was too much money. My questions to her were: What are you doing, putting gold down on the floor? What type of tubs did you ask for? Did you want to move walls? No, she only wanted to move a toilet and a tub. All right, that would mean new stack lines, unless we're within five feet of the stack. But the bottom line was that she was trying so hard to get this done by Christmas that she was losing patience and just didn't care anymore. She was about to hire the wrong people because she'd had enough of it.

You can't lose your patience. You must stay focused. It is your money. Do you realize how much it would cost to hire the wrong contractor and end up having to do the reno twice? The more you are in a hurry to get something done, the faster problems are going to arise. Just because you saw it in a magazine or on a television show, and said, "Oh my gosh, that kitchen is gorgeous," doesn't mean you can have it tomorrow.

Slow down. Educate yourself. Educate yourself to the point where you really understand what you're doing and what your contractor is saying, to the point that you're sick of it! Really, you can't take enough time to educate yourself. Slow down. Plan it right, then build it right, and you'll get it right the first time.

CHAPTER 2

The World Behind the Walls

Before you sink any money into a major kitchen or bath reno, you need to make sure that your plans (which might include tearing down walls, adding heavy granite counters, or installing a two-person soaker tub) can be supported—literally—by your house's structure. Here's why, and how, you should do an assessment of your home's structure.

The bones of the house

Here's why structure is so important: The frame in a house holds everything up. It acts like the bones in our body. A frame that's starting to sag means trouble. A house frame is full of joints and fasteners, and any weak points can act like a hinge. Weak points can happen because of age or previous "improvements." Any movement in the frame (through settling or failure of framing members) upsets the balance, and can cause a house to lean, bend, or tilt. This problem will get worse if nothing is done.

Every well-built house—whether old or new—starts out right: on a solid foundation, with structural and bearing walls level and true, and with point loads accurately calculated. And then someone (probably an enthusiastic DIYer who thinks they know what they're doing) renovates it. They cut out joists—or even beams—and compromise the structure. They make "educated" guesses about structural members, or about what the current bearing load on a wall is, or decide that some other wall can take a lot more load than it is taking.

And for a time you might not even notice, but believe me, the house is affected. The house might even undergo a second renovation—with more of the same types of changes to the structure. And what you end up with is cracks in the plaster, buckling drywall, windows and doors that stick—or, even worse, houses that lean, houses with floors that sag and slope, or houses that fall down.

During a renovation, a lot of people want to take down walls to create an open-concept floor plan, or just to get more space from an adjoining room. But what walls can you take down safely? I don't know how often I've been asked by people thinking about a renovation, "How do I know if it's structural?"

The truth is, you don't—and you don't have to. A good contractor knows. An architect knows, but it's a structural engineer who will need to redesign the load-bearing system. In fact any wall, even a load-bearing one, can be moved if it's done properly and the load points are recalculated and supported in other ways.

Even load-bearing walls can be removed if you want an open-concept kitchen, as long as you consult a structural engineer and make the necessary reinforcements to the structure.

Working with older houses

I love older houses. Many of the ones I've worked on show the skill and pride of the original craftspeople who built them. They're solid and have character, and in a good, mature neighbourhood, they have lasting value.

Another characteristic of older houses is that most of them have pretty straightforward structural layouts that aren't hard to figure out. The exterior walls support the perimeter, a beam supported by posts that you can see in the basement runs down the middle of the house, and the joists all run in the same direction from side to side. You could expect that the bearing walls are the outside walls, as well as the walls that are directly above the beam in the basement. The load was taken right down to the footing at the base of the foundation wall.

Just because your home is older doesn't mean it has a solid structure. I've seen some older houses that have terrible footings—sometimes they're just rubble or fieldstone foundations that are crumbling and falling in. In an old house with foundation problems a section of wall might give way or sink—then there's a domino effect. The leaning goes through the whole building.

It might not be the foundation. It might be that one or more of the sill beams (the wooden members that rest on the foundation, and that the rest of the structure is attached to) are rotted or damaged by insects (e.g., carpenter ants or termites), which will have the same effect on a wall as crumbled foundations. Or it could be structure that's been removed or weakened in previous renovations—one of the most common, and most serious, causes of problems in older houses. Tearing up a subfloor to discover the main support beams of a house were cut away to allow for some new plumbing is no laughing matter. I'd rather see an older house that's had no "improvements" than one that's full of fixes and crappy renovations done bit by bit over the years by a series of homeowners, or by people who want to flip the house and have no conscience about how they do it, or by incompetent handymen. That's why words like "fully updated" are red flags to ask questions when buying an older house.

Recently I was doing some work on a two-storey house that was originally a bungalow. When I removed the drywall ceiling and exposed the beam that held up half the second floor, I found the 14', 10" steel beam sitting on crumbling brick with no more than 2 inches of it carrying the weight. That was scary.

Lots of previous "improvements" will cost you money to repair before you can go forward with your plans. For instance, finding that a load-bearing wall has been taken out to "open up the space" between the kitchen and dining room means you'll need to re-support that load, probably affecting other rooms—or even other levels—of the house you hadn't planned to renovate.

Here's another reason why structural work should be done before renovations: repairing the structure can cause the house to shift slightly as it moves back into its correct position, which exerts torque on the walls and can cause them to crack. You want to deal with any effects of shifting before you spend all your money on finishing touches. Just imagine spending $30,000 to have custom cabinets professionally installed on old walls, and then doing structural repairs that cause your walls to shift. You might end up with damage to new cabinetry, or find that your cabinets no longer sit plumb and level on the wall, or the doors don't line up or close properly.

In any renovation, what really counts is what's behind the walls. If the structure is right, then your reno will last a long time.

There's a real cost to renovating when working with old construction. Retrofitting is always more expensive and more difficult than building new. Your contractor may find after starting the job that underneath some of the antique finishes, the house is too old, too rotten, or too compromised, and he'll have to tear back further than you expected—or budgeted for. Structural problems can be fixed, but usually at substantial cost.

If you're the owner of an older home, it's essential to have a thorough inspection done before proceeding any further with kitchen or bathroom plans. Do this inspection before you commit—either emotionally or financially—to the renovation project,

since you might need at least some of those renovation dollars for structural repairs. The contractor's or engineer's objective opinion might save you from a project that will be too costly or too big of a headache.

Structural issues with newer houses

In newer houses the floor plans are more complicated and structural plans are far more sophisticated than in older homes. Beams in the basement aren't just run down the middle of the house—sometimes a basement beam is installed to carry a point load only, and the real bearing takes another direction entirely on the second floor. Cantilevering—not that common in older homes—is used more and more today to carry loads in different directions, all of which requires careful engineering.

Material costs are rising, and builders reduce the size of beams and posts to the minimum required dimension and rely on a complex web of load-bearing members to do the structural work. It's just not that simple to figure out where the bearing points are anymore, or how much additional load you can add to any structure.

Some exterior walls can have so much glass in them they don't function as primary load-bearing walls anymore. In open-concept designs, there are beams where walls used to be. There are flush beams you can't see because they're inside the floor systems that carry loads where you think there are none.

What do you think happens when complicated designs like this meet with a shady, unqualified contractor? It may look great in the end, but you'll never know what's underneath—and unless you're experienced you won't even know what to look for. I came across one renovation where another contractor had cut out some tripled-up 2×10s (in other words, laminated beams) to run some new ducting to an addition. I'm surprised the house didn't fall down! I've seen beams that are just barely sitting in their beam pockets. Where there should be 4 to 6 inches of beam sitting firmly on the concrete or steel plate or wood post, I've seen as little as half an inch, on a cracked and weakened concrete block. It's not easy to catch because the beam pocket is always either covered over with drywall or parged over.

As with an older home, a newer home needs to be inspected structurally before renovations begin.

The critical areas for any house

A structural opinion can be offered by a structural engineer, an architect, or a reliable and experienced contractor. If the reno requires structural work, the municipal building and planning department will likely require an engineer's or architect's stamp, so your contractor will likely have to go to an engineer or architect for consultation and approval anyway. Whenever possible, get your hands on the original plans for the house and the plans for any subsequent renovations, and provide them to the engineer or contractor. But be aware that you can't always assume the house was actually built according to those plans. They should be used as a guideline only.

Here are some of the main areas that should be inspected before you get the green light for renovations:

- **The foundation should be inspected both inside and out, looking for any major cracks, bulges, leaning walls, or water damage.**
- **The wooden sill beam should be examined for signs of rot, water damage, or insect damage.**
- **Any beams should be examined for how firmly they're sitting in their beam pocket, how strong the pocket itself is, and whether the beams have been compromised by new plumbing, electrical, or HVAC work. Beams should also be checked to see that they're properly supported by posts, depending on the span.**
- **Joists in the basement should be inspected. Plumbing, electrical, and HVAC are the biggest culprits of damage to joists. Holes that are too large or placed too close to the bottom of the joist, as well as too many holes in one joist, can cause major structural problems.**

Efflorescence, the white buildup in this photo, generally isn't a problem, but it is evidence of moisture being present in walls and can lead to deterioration of the foundation. The bigger problem is that the vapour barrier is clearly not doing its job. There are holes in it, and it is not sealed properly at the bottom. Also, the black spots reveal either mould or air flow (and therefore poor insulation value).

What will need to be done?

Sections of the foundation wall may have to be repaired or replaced. Damaged sill beams will need to be replaced. If the damage was caused by water or insects, the source of the problem will have to be found—and dealt with. Beams that aren't resting securely in their pockets will need to be adjusted or replaced—a very big job. Beam pockets or other supports may need repairs as well.

For problems with joists, replacement joists may be required, or additional joists may have to be laminated (or "sistered") onto the old.

Extra vertical supports (such as new posts) may be required to help support a sagging structure. But you can't just throw a couple of jack posts in place. The building code requires proper footings under any post, which means breaking through the basement floor and pouring the necessary concrete footing. Only then can the post be set up.

The last word on structure

Any renovation that might have an impact on the structural integrity of your house should begin with a proper structural assessment. Kitchen and bathroom renovations are definitely in this category. The money you spend on a professional opinion is well worth the comfort of knowing what you've got, and that you did it right.

You may get bad news and find you need to do some structural repairs before you can go forward on your renovation. You may also find—scary but true—that your house or, more importantly, your family is in danger. The previous renovations may have compromised the structure to the point that you'll have to put your renovations on hold until you have properly re-supported your house. This could also be true about the roof, or the mechanical, plumbing, electrical, or ventilation. Count yourself lucky—better you know about problems up front and fix them now than spend thousands of dollars on a renovation and later find yourself with no more money to spend as you tear up a finished reno to undertake urgently needed repairs.

And remember: structural changes or repairs always—always—require a building permit. Never avoid this step. It's there to protect you, your family, and the investment of your home.

Plumbing and drainage

As with so many other aspects of your home, the plumbing you'll find behind the walls depends on the age of the building, since industry standards have changed over the years. You can figure out some things just by looking, if you're willing to take a trip down to your basement or check under your sinks. But before you can understand what you're seeing, you have to know a little about what you might find.

The plumbing of any house has two basic components: the supply lines (sometimes called the feed lines) and the waste lines or drains. Supply lines carry clean water from the main water intake pipe (which usually enters your house through the basement, well below the frost line) and take it to the various faucets and toilets in your home. Some newer homes may have a separate supply line for toilets that is fed by stored or collected rain water. This is a great water-saving measure, but unfortunately some municipalities don't permit it because the water isn't potable—that is, it's not safe for drinking. In many homes, all the water from your supply lines will go through a water softener of some kind, and then some of it will split off to the hot water heater. The waste lines take the water and waste from drains and toilets and deposit them into the main stack, which empties into a municipal sewer (or, in a rural area, into your septic system).

Drainage, waste, and ventilation

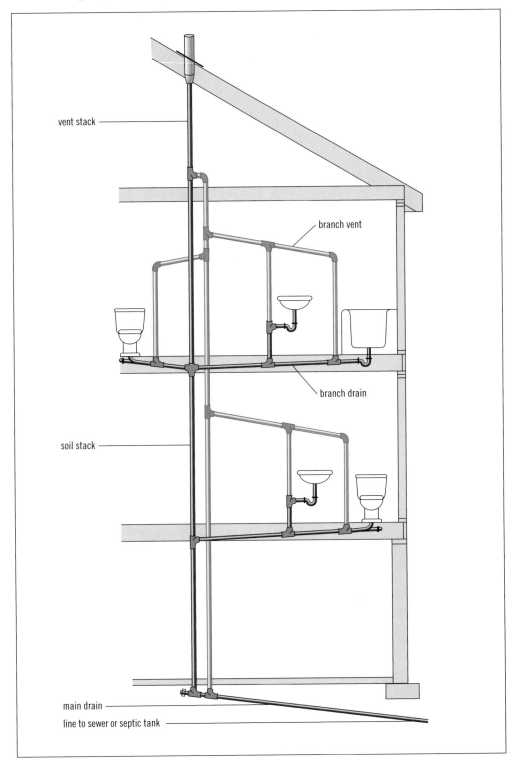

vent stack

branch vent

branch drain

soil stack

main drain

line to sewer or septic tank

Supply lines: lead, galvanized, copper—or something new?

For a long time, plumbing was made of lead. Over time, it became clear that lead was causing a lot of serious health problems, such as stillbirths and early deaths among infants. Thankfully, most municipalities switched over to galvanized steel for their water supplies as soon as they could, which was a big improvement, but some very old homes can still contain lead plumbing. If you suspect this is the case in your house, you should have it tested and replace it immediately if your suspicions are correct.

Galvanized steel is better than lead, but there are still a lot of problems with it. Because galvanized steel can't repel minerals in the water, scale builds up inside and reduces the amount of water that can pass through. Homeowners see this problem in reduced water pressure, and sometimes in discoloured water coming out of the pipes. The other problem with galvanized is that it can corrode and rust, which means that weak spots can suddenly burst. And, in the early years of galvanized, some of the zinc applied to the pipes contained lead, which is almost as risky for your health as having lead pipes. If you've still got galvanized supply lines in your house, you definitely want to have those replaced during your kitchen or bathroom renovation.

For supply lines, copper has been the standard material since the 1940s. If your house was built since that time, or has been substantially renovated since then, chances are you're going to find copper supply lines. That's basically a good thing. Although today there is yet another major change happening in the industry as plumbers move towards flexible plastic tubing, there's nothing really wrong with copper. It doesn't allow minerals to build up inside the lines, and it's a clean, nontoxic product that's safe for our water. It's relatively flexible and easy to work with, but it does require a lot of time for fitting and soldering joints, which is expensive when you're paying for a highly skilled plumber.

If your bathroom and kitchen layout isn't going to change during your reno, and if you want to take a conservative approach, there may be aspects of the plumbing that don't need to change. Look for signs of leakage and water damage around any plumbing, since this might tell you if it's time to replace the plumbing behind the walls.

The next question is, what should you replace your plumbing with? I like the new standard of flexible plastic tubing, which is a fantastic technology. The lines are flexible, and very few junctions are needed. A single manifold in the basement can have dedicated feed lines for each faucet, shower, or toilet in the house, and each one can have its own shut-off, which is a great safety feature. Or you can have a shut-off for each zone of the house (like individual floors). The flexible plastic tubing system works great with an on-demand hot water system, which I also recommend. There are a lot of cheap on-demand systems on the market, so make sure you buy a high-quality system—you'll get what you pay for.

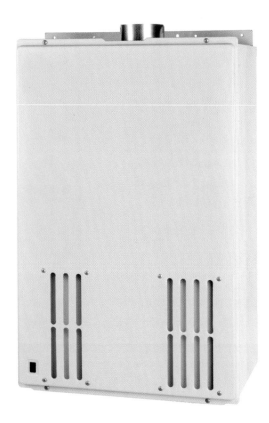

If you're not planning to replace all the plumbing in your house at one time, the flexible plastic tubing system can still work for you. You'll start with the manifold (probably in the basement) and just a couple of lines, then add more lines to the manifold as you renovate other rooms in your house and replace more plumbing lines.

Waste lines: Lead, cast iron, or plastic?

Every water-use location in your house—sinks, toilets, showers, and laundry—will have a drain that is connected to a main vent stack (larger houses will likely have a number of them). This vent stack is a hollow pipe that goes right through your roof, where gases can escape, and at the bottom it empties into the municipal sewer or septic tank.

In older homes it's still common to find vent stacks made of lead or cast iron. Generally you aren't as worried about lead in the waste lines, since the lead is only leaching into the waste water and not your drinking water, but it still ends up in the water system. But it might be time to replace that lead stack with ABS plastic piping. It won't corrode, and won't allow mineral scale to build up either.

Beyond the drains inside the house, the stack meets up with a line to your street that flows into the municipal sewer. The standard today is to use ABS pipe on all waste lines inside the house, and PVC pipe for any below grade (underground). In the past, clay pipe was often used for below-grade drainage, since it was the best thing available for a long time. The biggest problem with clay is that it breaks down over time, usually because tree roots wrap around it and cause it to crack or become clogged. The result can be a backup of the drains in your basement—not a pretty picture.

Don't forget about the drains!

If you're living in an older home, you may have clay lines running from your house to the street. Because these can break down and cause water to back up into your basement, I recommend that you have a camera inspection done by a professional—whether you've already had a serious backup problem or not. This is an especially important step if your property has large, mature trees anywhere near the house, since tree roots are a major cause of damage to clay pipes.

Tankless (on-demand) water heaters save energy, since they heat water as you use it. When switching to a tankless water heater, make sure you have the right size for your house. A big house may even need more than one water heater for adequate hot water supply.

MIKE'S TIP

Air behind water

Drains are something we rarely have to think about—until they don't work. When you wash a dish or flush a toilet, you take for granted that the waste and water will flow down the drain and out of your house. But when you plan a kitchen or bathroom renovation, drainage should be a key consideration.

One of the most important features in your home is the vent stack. Every fixture in your home—whether it's a sink, toilet, tub, or washing machine—needs to be connected to a vent stack (there is often more than one) to drain efficiently.

The stack is open at the top end, which extends about a foot above your roof. Drains work primarily by gravity, but in order to work properly, there needs to be air behind the water. Think of it this way: turn a pop bottle upside down, and the contents won't flow out quickly through the neck of the bottle. But punch a hole in the base, and the air helps force the pop out.

The vent stack also allows sewer gases to escape your home. Sewer gases aren't just foul-smelling—they can also pose a health hazard.

If your plans include moving or adding a fixture such as a kitchen sink, bathroom basin, or toilet, you need to know where the vent stack is located. If fixtures are more than five feet from the stack, you may need to run a separate vent line, which can add significantly to the cost of the renovation.

As a work-around, contractors may suggest installing an air admittance valve—better known as a cheater vent because you save a bit on the expense and labour of the plumbing job. Building codes don't allow these to be used for toilets, and I even avoid using them for sinks except as a last resort, like when a homeowner insists on putting a sink in a kitchen island.

If your sink is draining slowly, it may not be a clog. Improper venting could be the culprit. In fall, the stack's opening may be blocked by debris; in winter, a heavy snowfall may obstruct it. At the other end, tree roots can push against and even break metal pipe, and older clay pipe just breaks down over time.

Make sure the inspector time-stamps the video, notes at what distance from the house any potential obstructions are located, and makes a copy of the video for you to keep on file. If the sewer backs up after a heavy downpour and the city drains are at fault, you'll have a record of your drain's condition prior to the storm, which could help you get compensation for any damage.

If there's a problem with your clay tile drain, get it replaced with PVC before you have another backup. This is especially important to do before any expensive renos to the basement—such as adding a bathroom. Yes, you'll have to excavate, and the contractor might have to break up your basement floor to do the job right, but you won't regret it.

Inspecting your drains before you start a renovation is a good first step and can protect your investment.

If the drain looks good, I would check it again in two or three years. If it looks like there are breaks in the tile and a tree root or dirt is getting into the drain, but there's still no significant danger, check it again next year. Whatever you do, don't spend money on a basement bathroom without first making sure your drains are in good shape.

Electrical

I don't do my own electrical work, and neither should you, or anyone else who isn't a licensed electrical contractor. The worst renovation nightmares often involve bad electrical work because they endanger the lives of everyone in the home. Hiring a licensed electrical contractor is the only way to go in a renovation, as far as I'm concerned—I just wouldn't take the risk of going with anybody else.

As you do the assessment part of your research, it's also best to have a licensed electrical contractor do an inspection and inform you about the state of your electrical system.

Making your electrical right

The electrical component of any renovation has two parts. The first is determining what needs to be replaced to bring your electrical system up to code. The second is planning any upgrades or extras to satisfy your current and future electrical needs. The following questions will help you, together with a licensed electrical contractor, figure out how to do both.

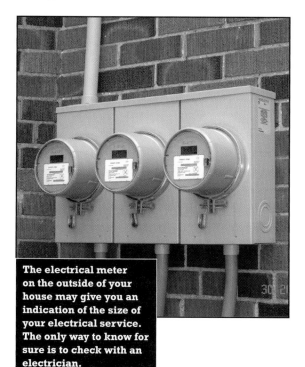

The electrical meter on the outside of your house may give you an indication of the size of your electrical service. The only way to know for sure is to check with an electrician.

How large is the service?

The wiring in your house carries 120 volts. But voltage won't tell you how much electricity is actually moving through a wire. That's amperage. Fuses and circuit breakers are rated in amperage. It's amperage you should be concerned about, because it's amps we talk about when we refer to the heart of the electrical system in your house: the main service panel.

The wiring in your house is just a collection of circuits that are routed through the main service panel. The panel brings the raw electricity into the house from the municipal lines (that's the heavy cable inside the box) and converts it into electricity that can be used for appliances, lights, etc.

There's a fuse or a circuit breaker for every circuit. Each circuit will have an amperage, usually 15 amps, and that circuit shouldn't be overloaded. A good rule of thumb is that you should have no more than 12 devices per 15-amp circuit. (A device can be anything from a switch receptacle to a light.) Bigger devices like air conditioners and stoves that use more electricity will have their own circuit.

The main service panel in older houses is often a fuse box. In newer homes, it's a panel of circuit breakers. Both work the same way. When you ask for too much electric current through a circuit by plugging in too many appliances, the fuse will burn out, or the circuit breaker will cut the connection. In this way the wire is kept from overheating and causing a fire.

If you have a 60-amp service to your house, it's probably not going to be adequate for your family's needs. You'll likely need 100 amps, but you might consider upgrading to 200 amps, depending on your plans for the future. If you have a lot of appliances, electronic equipment, plans for a hot tub or electric in-floor heating, or any plans to divide your home into two separate living units, a 200-amp service could be the way to go.

It can be difficult to tell how large the service is at your house. Circuit panels are hard to decipher, and the outside meter might or might not be correct. The most reliable way to tell? Ask a licensed electrical contractor.

How old is the wiring, and what kind is it?

Depending on the age of your home, and any renovations that may already have been done, you're likely to find one of three types of wiring: knob and tube, aluminum, or copper. I say likely because I have seen speaker wire used too! Obviously very wrong and very unsafe.

The earliest kind of wiring was knob and tube, and it was installed until about 1945. Knob-and-tube wiring was safe enough when it was first used, and still would be today except when it's mixed with newer wiring. New appliances require more power than older ones. Because the wires were designed for different amperages, you can easily overload an old knob-and-tube circuit—and start a fire. That's why today's minimum code—along with most insurance companies—requires that when renovating, knob and tube be replaced with copper wiring.

Aluminum wiring had a brief burst of popularity in the 1960s and 1970s. It was a good innovation at the time, but the move to copper wiring has meant that a lot of houses with aluminum wiring ended up, over the years, with a mix of copper and aluminum. Just like with knob and tube, it is mixing the different types of wires

MIKE'S TIP

Look for the signs.

What your electrician can't see—unless you open up the walls for your renovation—is whether there are any hidden junction boxes. Hidden junctions violate the electrical code, and for good reason: they're a big fire hazard.

If the electrical system looks like it's a hodgepodge of different types of wires, installed at various times over the years by people of varying levels of skill, you've got a pretty good clue that there could be some problems behind the walls. Seriously think about opening up those walls during the renovation to find out what else might be lurking back there.

that causes problems. For an aluminum system to be safe, it must be all aluminum—panel, receptacles, and switches. That's not very practical anymore, when the standard is copper.

The third and most common type of wiring you'll find, at least in any house built since the late 1970s, is copper. It's the industry standard, and by far the best conductor available.

Are there any junction boxes where you can see two different types of wire joined together?

Mixing different types of wires can cause serious safety issues. If your electrician sees this situation, they'll likely suggest changing the wiring on that circuit so that it's exclusively wired with copper.

What kind of outlets are currently in place?

If any electrical work has been done in recent years at your house, you probably have polarized outlets, and that's a good thing.

A polarized plug can only be inserted into an outlet one way. Basic household outlets have a hot side and a neutral side. A polarized plug ensures that the hot wire in your appliance can only be connected to the hot wire in the outlet. It's a safety feature, and you want to see that. The third prong you see on some plugs is the ground pin. It protects you even more from a severe shock caused by a faulty cord or malfunctioning appliance.

If your outlets have room for only two equal-size prongs, they're outdated and should be replaced during your renovation. These outlets are often an indicator that the wiring behind the wall is also outdated or inadequate. However, polarized plugs

GFCI outlets are required by code within three feet of a water source.

don't necessarily mean that you have updated wiring; it may just be a superficial change that's been made in recent years. A licensed electrical contractor will be able to tell you more.

The worst-case scenario

If your house has wiring that dates before the 1970s (either knob and tube or aluminum), your electrician may suggest that the whole thing needs to be upgraded. This may be a lot more than you bargained for—or budgeted for.

If you can't afford to replace the entire system at once, consider doing it in stages, beginning with a new service panel at an appropriate amperage level (at least 100 amps for today's lifestyles), and using all-new copper wiring for any circuits that will be affected by the kitchen or bathroom renovation. You can do other rooms as you renovate later on. In the long run, you may spend a bit more to rewire your house this way, but this may fit your budget better than trying to do a whole-house electrical job along with a major kitchen or bathroom reno.

Maybe you'll be lucky and find out that your home's basic wiring is okay and your electrician will only need to work on the wiring needed for your new kitchen or bathroom.

Whatever the case, make sure that your renovation takes all electrical issues into consideration and that you communicate your wishes clearly—both in your design drawings and in conversation. And, of course, make sure that you (or your general contractor) hire only a licensed electrical contractor to do the job. (See more about kitchen design and lighting starting on page 109.)

HVAC (heating, ventilation, and air conditioning)

When it comes to your heating and ventilation system, there are a few things that can tell you whether you've got problems that need to be addressed before or during your kitchen or bathroom renovation.

Evaluating a forced-air system

First of all, you want to look at the age of your furnace. There's often a label with a date on the front panel or just inside the front panel. You won't hurt yourself by looking inside, but make sure the main switch is off before you remove the panel. If a forced-air furnace is more than 15 years old, it's starting to get old and probably isn't working as efficiently as it did when it was new.

How your furnace looks is also an indication of how well it's doing. Is it clean inside? Is it rusty? Is there a sticker indicating when it was last cleaned or had a routine maintenance check?

When looking at the ventilation system—that is, the system of metal ductwork that runs throughout the home, bringing hot (or cool) air into the rooms, and also returning air to the furnace for heating or cooling—the most important thing is to notice whether it's been "contaminated" by previous renovations that might have been done badly. Are there new runs coming off old ones (new pipes attached to old)? If changes were made since the house was built, especially if an addition has been built onto the house, was the work done by a qualified HVAC specialist? Were permits taken out for the work, and was it inspected by the local municipal building inspector?

Finally, when thinking about your HVAC prior to renovating, ask yourself some really obvious questions. How comfortable are your rooms? Are there hot or cold spots that may not be due to a problem with insulation or a window? Is the temperature balanced between upstairs and downstairs?

An HVAC specialist can check air flow to better balance the heating and cooling throughout your house.

An HVAC specialist is the best person to assess your forced-air system. They can do a test to determine if the airflow in your home is efficient and balanced, and they can tell you if any changes that were previously made to the system are up to par. If there are problems, a renovation is definitely the time to address them.

If your kitchen or bath reno involves adding on to your home, or building into space that was previously unfinished, keep in mind that your furnace and air conditioning system may be affected. Furnaces must be the right size for the space being heated, and your current furnace—even if it's still relatively new and in good shape—may not be adequate for the expanded footprint of your home. Again, an HVAC specialist can advise you on what you need.

In a bathroom, you're more likely to be concerned about having enough heat for comfort, while in the kitchen heat isn't usually as much of an issue because cooking and baking generate heat. Air conditioning is often the bigger concern in a kitchen. But for both rooms you want to make sure you've got adequate heat and adequate cooling.

I've often seen a really big mistake made in bathroom renos: the homeowner or contractor wants to reconfigure the space, but instead of moving the heating vent, they take the easy way out and just cover it over. You're left without heat or cool air in your bathroom!

If it's really too difficult to move the air vent (or the air return, if there is one in the bathroom), you still need to have a heat source, and you could consider an electric radiant floor heating system. It's installed over your subfloor and before your finish floor. It's comfortable underfoot, and it now uses less electricity than you might think.

In both bathrooms and kitchens, removing moist air is one of the biggest ventilation challenges. Installing high-quality, efficient, and quiet fans is the solution, and this is one area where you don't want to go cheap. Moisture that stays in the air will lead to problems with mould and mildew and all the unhealthy side effects that go along with them.

Both kitchen and bathroom fans should be exhausted directly

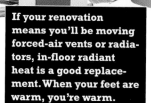

If your renovation means you'll be moving forced-air vents or radiators, in-floor radiant heat is a good replacement. When your feet are warm, you're warm.

to the outside, either through the roof of the house or through an exterior wall, and the exhaust line must be insulated to reduce any possibility of condensation being created as it goes through an unheated space such as the attic. You do not want moisture—and all the possible consequences, such as mould, rot, and dampened insulation—in your attic.

You always need good ventilation in a bathroom to help prevent mould. Don't skimp on a ventilation fan, and make sure it's vented outside, not to an attic.

If you have old-style radiant heat

If you have a boiler and hot water radiator system in your home instead of a forced air furnace, you can expect the boiler to last for 25 to 35 years or even more—it's not uncommon to hear of 50-year-old boilers. That's one advantage of the old-style radiant heat. However, with a system like this you won't have ductwork as you would with forced air, and that means you don't have a built-in system for central air conditioning.

A renovation is the perfect time to consider your air conditioning options. The priciest and most disruptive option is to have ductwork installed so you can run a forced air system through it. That's going to mean changes to a lot of rooms, and adding bulkheads to conceal the ductwork in some places—which may not suit the character of an older home. There are newer air conditioning systems that can be installed, such as the ductless "mini-split" air conditioners that have the compressor on the outside of the house and one or more louvered, wall-mounted units on the inside. Another option is to retrofit the house with a high-velocity duct system. Because the lines are only 2 to 4 inches in diameter, they can be added to the walls in much the same way that a central vacuum system would be. One drawback to the high-velocity system is that noise will be more of an issue, though some higher-priced systems are designed to minimize noise.

As you plan your renos, you might be looking at changing the layout of your kitchen or bathroom. Maybe those changes will mean that one or more of your old hot water radiators is now in the way. Can you work around that? Yes, but keep in mind that adding, subtracting, or moving a cast iron radiator is a fairly big job. All the water has to be drained from the system, and there's always the possibility that a radiator will crack when being moved, which would make it useless.

And remember: if you want to remove a radiator from the system, you should be replacing the heat source with something else. Radiant in-floor heat can be the best solution. Either a water-based system or an electric system is great, since they can be installed under most types of flooring, and will give you a floor that's warm and comfortable at all times. The beauty of in-floor heating is that if your feet are warm, the rest of you feels warm too. You can actually keep your room at a lower temperature and still feel more comfortable than you would with forced air heat.

Another alternative to moving an old cast iron radiator is to replace it with a wall-mounted radiator. This newer generation of radiators take up less floor space and look nice and sleek. However, they should only be used if you're going to replace all the radiators in the house. The reason is that the two different kinds of radiators require different temperatures from your boiler if they're going to run properly, so they don't mix well.

Needless to say, any changes to your radiant heat system should be done only by a qualified HVAC specialist, preferably one with lots of radiant heat experience.

Insulation

Knowing what kind of insulation you have in your walls—as well as in the attic and basement—is the basic starting point if you're thinking of upgrading your home's insulation during a renovation. Insulation is critical to how a house functions—it makes the rooms more comfortable and it keeps heating and cooling costs down. If you start by insulating even one room (such as the kitchen or a bathroom), you'll notice a difference in the comfort level of that room immediately. And if the bathroom or kitchen shares a wall with an office or bedroom, soundproofing with insulation is also a great idea.

MIKE'S TIP

Removing asbestos and UFFI is NOT a DIY project!

Asbestos is a natural mineral with an amazing ability to resist high temperatures. That's what makes it such a good insulator, and that would be good news if it weren't also a known carcinogen (cancer-causing agent). Asbestos is harmless if it's left alone, but when it's disturbed and the fibres are let loose in the air, some fibres can find their way into human lungs and cause severe lung impairment or cancer. Asbestos was banned as an insulator in the 1980s.

In vermiculite insulation that was installed prior to the 1980s, asbestos can still sometimes be found. As long as the installed vermiculite isn't moved, it won't harm you, but if you have it in your attic and you're about to undergo a renovation that will disturb it, you need to have it tested and removed. Prior to the late 1970s, asbestos was added to drywall compound as well, which makes even demolition of older houses a job that can be hazardous to your health. Old linoleum floors may also contain asbestos, and they should be tested before being removed during a renovation. Often these floors are left in place and new flooring material is installed over top. Wrong! This is exactly the time to get the flooring out of your house—but hire professionals to do it.

UFFI (urea formaldehyde foam insulation) contains high levels of formaldehyde. It off-gasses into the air and can cause health problems in humans, though it becomes harmless after it cures. Still, if it gets wet it can start to break down and then it needs to be removed. It was also banned in Canada in 1980.

If your home contains any asbestos-based product or UFFI—your contractor should be able to tell you if that's possible, and tests can confirm it—it should be removed. But don't ever try to do this yourself. There are certified removal professionals who should be called in for a job like this.

How can you tell what kind of insulation you've got—if any? You can't see behind the walls. A home inspector or contractor with a thermographic imaging camera can. You can make some logical deductions about insulation based on the age of your house, though. If you've got quite an old house that hasn't been substantially renovated, there may not be any insulation at all, or maybe just some old newspapers stuffed into the wall cavities—and you'd be surprised how many of these homes still exist in a country as cold as Canada.

How can this be? Well, think about it: having walls that leaked heat wasn't much of a problem in an era of cheap fuel because you could just keep pumping more heat out of your furnace and not worry about heat loss. But when fuel prices skyrocketed in the 1970s, everyone became a little more energy conscious and people began to think twice about how well insulated their homes were.

Of course, there was some insulation being used prior to the 1970s, but most of it was being installed in factories, schools, and office buildings, not in people's homes.

Cellulose insulations (using fibres from wood, straw, cotton, or other living cells) are among the earliest types of insulation and they're still in use today. Glass foam and glass fibre insulations (in batts) began to be developed and sold in the late 1930s, and they're still the most popular type of residential insulation on the market; they're fairly cheap, and they can be installed by just about anyone. After the Second World War, there were many new products introduced, including rock wool insulations and diatomaceous silica products.

Asbestos was a popular insulating material for many decades, until researchers determined that it was a dangerous, cancer-causing substance. Thankfully, most of the asbestos insulation out there was used in factories and public buildings, and over the last thirty years or so almost all of it has been removed and replaced with safer alternatives.

Along with asbestos, another unfortunate attempt at insulating happened with UFFI. This was developed in the 1950s, and because it could be blown onto walls in liquid form it was valued for its ability to insulate difficult-to-reach cavities in house walls. Many Canadians insulated their homes with UFFI during the 1970s, but it was banned in Canada in 1980 because of health concerns. It's not the same thing as today's polyurethane foam insulation, which in fact is the product I recommend most highly.

The bottom line, as far as I'm concerned, is that insulation is one of the most important factors in taking your home to a comfortable, energy-efficient level, a level that is more valuable in today's energy-conscious marketplace.

You have different insulation options depending on whether you open your walls to the studs during the reno or leave the walls intact and use some form of retrofit insulation. Insulating an older home requires some understanding of your home and how it was built. Making a home airtight may create newer and even larger problems than anticipated, like getting the vapour barrier wrong or sealing the house without providing a way for air exchange.

Insulation options if you're gutting

Opening up walls during a reno gives you the ideal opportunity to choose from any type of insulation. The best insulation on the market can only be installed on open studs—that means either during new construction, or during a reno that takes the walls back to the studs.

The right time to insulate

Here's a really important piece of advice: make sure your electrical work is done before having any type of spray foam applied to the studs. It's very difficult to get wiring through the studs after insulating with foam, since the studs will be pretty much covered up. Same goes for rough plumbing (such as flexible tubes), and anything else that might need to be run through the studs. Think ahead!

For my money there's only one type of insulation to buy, and that's a closed-cell polyurethane foam insulation that's sprayed on in liquid form and expands to fill every possible gap. It creates what's called "intimate contact," meaning that there are no holes or gaps left between the insulation and the surface it's applied to. It doesn't just slow down the movement of air through the wall cavities, it stops it altogether. There should be no air leaks once this foam is sprayed onto your walls. But be aware that all polyurethane foam is not created equal! There's closed-cell polyurethane and open-cell polyurethane. There's a big difference. Open-cell is softer, relies on air for insulation, and provides less R-value. It's lighter, at between ½ and ¾ pounds per cubic foot, whereas closed-cell is between 2 and 3 pounds per cubic foot. Open-cell is cheaper per cubic foot and per unit of R-value, but its effectiveness is reduced if it gets wet. I don't think it holds up well in the long run compared to closed-cell.

There's no doubt that closed-cell spray-foam insulation—or any insulation that requires someone other than your contractor to install it—will cost you more than other types of insulation. It's about three times the cost of fibreglass batts, for example, which are probably the most commonly used, especially by DIYers. But there really is no comparison between the insulating value of foam versus fibreglass, and you'll quickly see the difference in lower fuel bills when you have spray-foam insulation applied. Insulation is usually priced by the square foot, installed. Most insulation contractors will set a minimum price for any job, so having a very small area to insulate doesn't mean your costs will be lower—in fact, they could be higher than expected. Don't be surprised if your local municipal inspector asks for a vapour barrier when using closed-cell spray foam. If so, your contractor should be able to get the necessary technical data to show why it's not needed.

If you just can't find the money for the best insulation, of course there are other options out there—though none of them have the same insulating value. You can use rock wool, fibreglass batts, or newer, "greener" denim batts. If you use batts of any kind, make sure they're properly installed (not forced into a space that's too small, or

What is R-value?

Simply put, R-value is a measure of how well a material—usually insulation—resists heat loss. Basically, the higher the R-value, the better the material insulates.

As useful as R-value can be in helping you choose insulating materials, it doesn't tell the whole story. For one thing, R-value performance tests assume no air leakage. If you don't protect your walls properly against air leakage, you've wasted your money.

Moisture also has an effect on R-value. Many types of insulation use trapped air to do the job. Moisture—even a small amount—can make the material compress and lose that trapped air, reducing the insulating material's effectiveness to only one-quarter of its rated R-value.

Exceeding R-value isn't everything. What matters is the product you use and the way it's installed. Insulation that provides a thermal break, like spray foam, is always better than one that only provides a thermal barrier, like batt insulation.

with gaps left in larger stud spaces), with a vapour barrier that's Tuck-taped to seal off every possible air leak. There are lots of rigid foam products available as well, but these are best used in the basement to give you that thermal break you need as a starting point. Rigid foam is also ideal on the exterior, in combination with fibreglass batts or cellulose fibre insulation on the inside.

Insulation options on existing walls

Let's say you've decided not to gut your kitchen or bathroom. Maybe you recently had all the electrical in your house updated or your plumbing replaced without tearing out the walls entirely, and you don't want the added cost of new drywall. Or maybe you love the look of your old plaster and lath walls, and you don't want to destroy them. Whatever the reason might be for keeping your old walls intact, you still need to ensure that you have enough insulation.

When you don't remove the finish layer of your walls (plaster and lath, plaster and gypsum board, or drywall) as you renovate, your insulation choices are more limited, and you'll never reach the insulating value that you could with open walls. There are still some types of insulation that can be blown into existing wall cavities. The least expensive option is a cellulose fibre. It's often made from recycled newsprint, and treated with chemicals to resist fire and settling of the fibres. Installers will drill small holes into each stud cavity (every 16 inches), use a hose to blow the fibres into the

Installed by pros, closed-cell spray-foam is the best choice for insulation.

cavity, and then fill the holes with a wood plug and some drywall mud. The homeowner has the responsibility of sanding the holes and repainting them to match the wall. Repainting the walls entirely is often needed for the cleanest finish.

The disadvantages of cellulose fibre is that its R-value isn't as high as other forms of insulation (only about 3 to 3.5 R per inch), and it has a tendency to settle over time, which reduces its effectiveness even further. It doesn't have a vapour barrier either, so moisture can get into the wall cavities and cause mould. But if cellulose fibre in the walls is paired up with an exterior renovation that includes a layer of rigid foam insulation properly Tuck-taped to prevent moisture from entering, it can be a good enough solution.

Blown cellulose insulation is a good alternative for attics, and you should make sure you have enough insulation there—no matter what other renos you happen to be doing. The more insulation you have in the attic, the better—at least 12 inches of blown fibres, but preferably 24 inches or even more. It should create a "blanket" to block warm air from escaping into the attic and through the roof. But it's also very important to make sure the insulation doesn't block the vents in the soffits—these are critical for letting your attic breathe. Basically you want your attic to be a cold zone, with no transfer of that cold air into the heated areas of your home.

MIKE'S TIP

Spray foam is not for finished walls.

I'm a big fan of spray foam, but I always use it when walls are open so we can ensure you get an intimate contact and there aren't any gaps. It's pretty tempting to try a similar product that claims to do the same job at a fraction of the cost, like Retrofoam, since your installer just drills holes in the wall and sprays it in. Retrofoam is legal in the United States, but not in Canada. It was blocked by Health Canada, unfortunately not before over 700 homeowners had Retrofoam installed in their homes. Make sure you know what's going into your house, do your homework, and don't be afraid to ask your contractor what is being used.

Windows

When assessing the scope of your renovation, the first question to ask about windows is, do they need to be replaced?

As you know, I'm in favour of doing things right the first time, so I'd rather not see a kitchen renovation that involves new cabinetry, a new tiled backsplash, and all kinds of fancy touches—while you leave the 25-year-old windows in place.

Think about it: why would you spend so much to finish the room properly, when you'll probably have to replace those windows in a few years? A good replacement job means removing the whole window, right back to the stud opening, and repairing any problems with moisture, rot, etc., before installing the new window. Don't risk damage to your new cabinets, tiles, counters, or anything else. Replace nearly worn-out windows during your renovation.

It's true that sometimes windows don't need replacement. It depends on the age and quality of the window. Before you make the decision about whether or not to replace, here are some things to know about windows.

Every window leaks heat—no matter how good a window is, its R-value can't compete with an insulated wall. Heat leaks in and out—in winter, the warm air inside wants to escape through the glass, and in summer, the heat from outside is trying to get in. Year-round, UV light passes through the glass. Replacing windows will probably improve your home's energy efficiency.

Old windows were made with a single pane of glass, set in a wooden frame and secured with putty. Things improved when storm windows were placed over these, which created an air layer between the two windows and helped with insulation. Later windows had double-glazing—two sheets of glass together in the frame. Many older homes still have single- or double-glazed windows, and they lose a lot of heat. It's almost like having an open hole in your wall. I would strongly recommend replacing any windows like these.

The newer generation of quality windows have an inert gas injected between the layers of glass. This helps provide insulation and almost doubles the R-value of a window. Low-E glass stands for "low-emissivity" glass. This has been treated with a microscopic metallic oxide spray that cuts down the UV light passing through the glass. It lets in light, but reflects heat in summer and helps retain it in winter. If your home already has windows like this and there are no mechanical problems with the opening mechanisms, or any signs of rot or decay around the window frame due to improper installation, you probably don't need to replace them.

If you decide to replace

You can get windows in many architectural styles to suit your home, and in a variety of materials to suit your budget. You can find wood-framed windows, aluminum windows, fibreglass windows, and all-vinyl windows in a variety of designs and styles: single-hung or double-hung, vertical or horizontal sliders, casement, etc.

My favourite kind of window is an awning style that allows you to keep the window open when it rains.

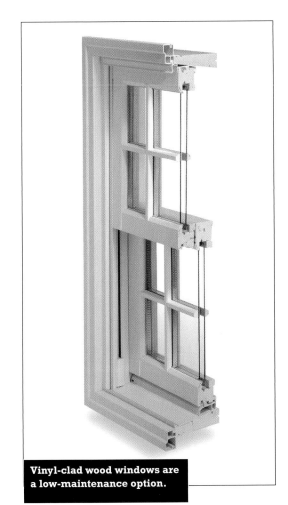

Vinyl-clad wood windows are a low-maintenance option.

Wood-framed windows are beautiful, but they can be high maintenance and will need to be repainted or treated regularly. A wood-framed window will expand and contract a lot if it's in direct sunlight for any part of the day, and it will lose its paint as a result.

Another option is wood-clad windows with vinyl exteriors. They provide more weather resistance and need less maintenance, and you'll still have the look of wood on the inside. With a lower-quality vinyl-clad window you can have problems with water getting under the vinyl and rotting the wood.

I prefer high-quality vinyl windows to metal or wood: vinyl is easier to clean, it lasts longer than metal, and it needs less maintenance than wood.

Windows by the kitchen sink are a must for most homeowners. A bump-out window can add more light and even more counter space, but it's like a mini-addition in itself if you're enlarging the window because it affects the structure of your house.

Letting the light in:
Adding or enlarging windows

Which would you rather live in: a dark, windowless house, or a house filled with daylight? That's a no-brainer. A renovation is the time to assess the natural light situation in your kitchen or bathroom, and make changes if necessary. Ask yourself the following questions:

Are you happy with the amount of light the room gets?

Even if you think you have enough light, consider whether more would be better. Not only is natural light probably the best form of light, it's also the least expensive and most energy-conscious option.

Could changes to your landscaping improve the amount of light that enters the room?

This is an obvious point, but sometimes people forget that overgrown shrubs or trees can block out valuable light. Consider whether the greenery can be pruned back or removed altogether and replaced with lower-growing plants.

MIKE'S TIP

Window installation is critical.

No matter how good the window you buy, if it's not installed properly it's not worth much. It will leak air—and possibly water—and cost you money.

Make sure your installer is a professional. If it's a replacement window job, make sure they remove the old window completely and clean out to the rough stud opening before they try to install the new window. Be sure they check for any damage or rot, and repair it before they finish the installation. And, most important, make sure they insulate the window properly with low-expanding spray foam (high-expanding foam can expand too much and keep the window from operating properly) to eliminate drafts.

When it comes to windows, like most things, you get what you pay for. Whatever type of window you choose, make sure you buy high-quality thermal ones with a good R-value. And most important, make sure they're properly and professionally installed.

How will you deal with privacy?

If your house is on a busy street, or you just don't like to feel that your family life is on display to people walking by, adding windows may not be a good option. You'll spend a lot of money, only to feel that you need to cover the windows most of the time to keep prying eyes away.

In bathrooms, privacy always has to be a consideration—unless you live in the woods and aren't worried about the passing wildlife getting a view. For bathroom windows, a pebbled finish or some other type of translucent finish will still allow some light to enter while blocking the view. I prefer windows that are operable, so I suggest avoiding glass blocks, but they can be a good alternative for a basement bathroom that's outfitted with a top-quality fan for ventilation.

Will adding or enlarging a window mean giving up too much valuable wall space?

Storage is a key component of both kitchens and bathrooms, and wall space is needed for cabinetry. Be realistic about how much wall space you need before giving it up to a larger window.

If the room you're renovating is the kitchen, what direction(s) does it face?

Many people like to have a sunny kitchen in the morning, so east- or south-facing walls should be outfitted with as many windows as possible. Windows on a north-facing wall can expose your kitchen to a lot of winter cold, so you might want to be conservative about windows to the north. Likewise, late-afternoon sun can be too strong for comfort, so if you have west-facing walls you'll want to balance your desire for sunset views with a practical concern for the amount of light and radiant heat that will invade your kitchen.

Can windows be added or enlarged with minimal exterior changes?

Vinyl-sided or wood-sided houses can be modified somewhat more easily and less expensively than houses with brick exteriors. No matter what, there will be costs to adding or enlarging windows, since both the interior and exterior will be affected. If you choose this route, you need to make sure that your contractor gets the right permits (permits are *always* needed to add or enlarge a window because it changes the structure of the house) and supports the house above the window opening.

Large windows with a view are good in a kitchen when you're not giving up needed storage space.

Skylights—another alternative to bring in light

I love skylights—they're a great way to bring natural light into your home. They're "green" features because they allow you to switch off your lights in the daytime and reduce energy use. Skylights actually can provide over three times as much light as a vertical window of the same size, because light from directly above is stronger than light from the horizon.

They come in a huge variety of sizes and styles, in acrylic or glass, clear or tinted. Whatever your design style, you can probably find a skylight to suit it. A skylight is basically a hole in your roof, with a window in it. But if it's not installed properly and professionally you will have the worst of both window and roof problems—condensation, heat loss, summer overheating, and leaks. If you choose a skylight for your kitchen or bathroom renovation, make sure it's installed 100% correctly by a pro—there's no room for error when you're making a hole in your roof.

Keeping the outside out

People often ask me about skylights. They're nervous about adding one because they've heard they leak. If your skylight is a good-quality one and has been professionally installed, it's not likely to leak.

Curb-mounted skylights—whether glass or plastic—are a smart choice because they place the skylight higher than the surface of the roof. The skylight is then flashed properly, which seals it and prevents the roof from leaking.

Often people find water damage they think comes from a leaky skylight and it turns out the cause is condensation build-up. Just like windows on your walls, windows in the roof—your skylights—can gather moisture from the air in your home and form frost on the inside of your skylight in winter. But instead of pooling on a windowsill, the water will drip onto your floors, or run down ceilings and walls. This problem is caused by poor air circulation and too much humidity in your house, or by windows that aren't very energy efficient—when cold air meets warm, condensation is the result.

Air leakage siphons about half an average home's heating and cooling energy to the outdoors. Air leakage through windows is responsible for much of this loss. Well-designed windows have durable weatherstripping and high-quality closing devices that effectively block air leakage.

Skylights can be a source of heat loss as your warm inside air escapes through the roof in winter. And in summer they can create a lot of solar heat gain—which might cost you since you've got to run your air conditioning to compensate. Tinted or light-reflective glass will reduce overheating, but it may also reduce the amount of daylight that comes in. Louvered blinds can be installed to direct the light but still let it in.

You might be scared of adding skylights because of stories of them leaking, but properly installed skylights (like the ones you see here to the left and right of the range hood) don't leak and can help with airflow in your house.

If you get a skylight that can open, use it! Hot air builds up near the ceilings—opening a skylight releases the hot air, and allows cooler air to be pushed up from below. In fact, some architects actually design houses with this silo effect in mind, but for most people's homes, the tendency for hot air to rise (convection) means that upper-level rooms can become too hot in summer, and lower-level rooms can be hard to heat in winter.

A skylight will never be as well insulated as your roof. It can't be. But a well-made skylight can minimize both heat loss in winter and heat gain in summer. Most skylights are now made with Low-E glass for greater thermal efficiency.

Tubular skylights

Tubular skylights are even better than traditional ones. You can use them in any room that has roof access—even closets—and you rarely have to remove roof structure to put them in.

Tubular skylights are quick and inexpensive to install because they don't need the same amount of construction as regular skylights. The tube just fits between roof trusses and rafters, so it can be installed with minimal structural change. Basically, it captures sunlight or daylight on the roof and redirects it down a highly reflective tube into the room below. A diffuser spreads the light evenly throughout the room.

To light more than one room with this method, you don't have to create a dome forest on your roof. One square cut-out in the roof can feed several tubes into different rooms. You can install incandescent or fluorescent lights or, even better for energy conservation, LED lights into the tube for night time.

As with any opening in your roof, proper installation is absolutely critical to avoid moisture damage from leaks or condensation.

Following up: Checklist

After a thorough assessment of your house, you should know about the repairs and upgrades your home needs either before or during your kitchen or bathroom reno. You should also have some idea about how each of the areas we looked at will be affected by a renovation.

Now it's time to make some decisions. For each area—structure, plumbing, electrical, HVAC, insulation, and windows—use the following checklist to help you keep track of the details of your reno. You can keep coming back to this checklist, and others in the book, as you get closer to a finished plan. Your final list will be important to pass on to your general contractor and any subcontractors working on the job.

Structure

Condition of foundation:

_____

Condition of sill beams:

_____

Condition of joists/posts/framing:

_____

Repairs needed:

_____

Plumbing and drainage

Type and condition of existing supply and waste lines:

_____

Type and condition of existing vent stack:

_____

Upgrades and/or additions needed (e.g., on-demand hot water system):

_____

Special circumstances or fixtures (e.g., extra prep sink in kitchen):

_____

Condition of drainage around foundation (look for evidence of moisture in basement):

_____

Upgrades or repairs needed:

_____

Electrical

Size (amperage) of electrical service:

_____

Type of existing wiring:

_____

Upgrades and/or additions needed:

_____

Special circumstances or appliances (e.g., fans, electric range, bathtub with jets):

_____

Possible future needs:

_____

HVAC

Type of existing heat system and fuel source:

_____

Add to or modify existing ductwork?

_____

Add alternative source of heat (e.g., in-floor heat)?

_____

Insulation

Type and amount of existing insulation:

_____

New or additional insulation needed?

_____

Type:

_____

Total square footage:

_____

Windows

Replace, enlarge, add?

_____

Number and type(s) of windows:

_____

Size(s):

_____

CHAPTER 3

Hiring Right and Working with Your Contractor

A good general contractor is the key to a successful renovation. There's no two ways about it: the general contractor you hire has the power to make or break the outcome of your reno. It's worth every bit of time and effort it takes to find the right person because it will affect your home, your pocketbook, and even your health.

A bad general contractor, on the other hand, costs you money—sometimes, a lot of it. They could leave you with a reno that's so badly done your house is actually worth *less* than before the work started. I've heard and seen too many examples of how a bad contractor has almost cost people their home and their marriage. A bad general contractor can cause damage to your property, not to mention the damage that's harder to see: the time you'll spend dealing with the problems; the disruption to your life and the frustration, anger, and disappointment. You were looking forward to great results, not pain and suffering.

In the following pages, I'm going to tell you how to find a good general contractor, how to put together a contract that protects you, and how to be the kind of client who gets great results.

First, let's be clear about what I mean when I say "general contractor."

A general contractor will either do or contract out all the work on your job. They will find out what you want; come up with a plan, budget, and timeline for getting it done; and oversee the whole project from start to finish. The general contractor will find and hire anyone needed for the job, from designers and engineers to carpenters, drywallers, electricians, plumbers, etc. The general contractor will also do all the scheduling so that the subcontractors (tradespeople) complete their part of the job on time, smoothly paving the way for the next trade. The general contractor is your go-to person, the one who deals with any problems or questions along the way.

There are other kinds of contractors too. Specialty contractors make their living doing specific jobs, such as kitchen or bathroom renovations. For electrical, plumbing, and heating and cooling work, you need a trade contractor. You should always go with someone who is licensed. In every province and territory in Canada, there are different licensing requirements for people who work in the trades. Your provincial government's website should be able to direct you to information on licensing in your region.

What you really need to ask

Here are some general questions to ask any contractor you're thinking of hiring, no matter what the job. Remember, I always say that finding a good contractor can take as long—or longer—than doing the job itself.

How long have you been in business?
A longer time (measured in years, not months) usually indicates that the general contractor is experienced, and good enough to stay in business. And how long have they and their company been around? If they've been in business for twenty-five years but their company has only been incorporated for one year, that's a bad sign. What did they do previously? Did they change company names to avoid being sued?

Are you licensed and insured? Do you make sure all your employees and subcontractors are also insured, and licensed whenever a license is required? Can you provide proof of insurance and licensing in writing?
This is critical, and the proof of licensing and insurance is something that will become part of any contract you sign.

Can you give me some names of past customers that I can call for references?
Ask for at least five or six references—the more the better, don't be shy. This is your house and your money. Your job now is to contact (or, when possible, visit) the

references. You'd be surprised how many people make the mistake of not doing this. If a contractor is unable or unwilling to provide you with references, cross them off your list. Once you make contact with the references, ask lots of questions. Was the contractor on time, were they professional, did they call you back quickly, did they leave the site clean every day, was there a good team of tradespeople on the job? Have you had any problems with your reno? Did it cost more than budgeted? Why?

Do you have any ideas or suggestions about this project?

If the contractor's a pro, they'll probably be thinking of ways to make your project work better or give you better value for your money.

Can I get a ballpark figure?

The contractor won't be able to give you a hard-and-fast estimate at first glance, but they should be able to give you a general idea. Just keep in mind that this needs to be done carefully. Avoid price comparisons if you can see that the work being offered (including materials and skill set) isn't comparable from one contractor to the next.

When could you start and how long do you think it would take?

Most contractors worth the money aren't available at a moment's notice. Be suspicious if they say they can start tomorrow.

Getting quotes

Once you've interviewed and checked references, you'll have a short list. Time to get down to dollars and cents. The trick here is to make sure everyone is bidding on the same thing. It's your responsibility to make sure the information is the same for every contractor. If you don't provide adequate plans and specifications, each contractor will decide how they'll carry out the work and what materials they'll use. That's going to give you an "apples and oranges" situation, and that's no good for anybody.

First, you need plans and specifications so that each contractor can quote on the same thing. Plans include the drawings, diagrams, or sketches that describe the work to be done. These drawings will also be required to obtain a building permit. You could hire a registered designer, architect, or even a general contractor to draw up plans (which would mean paying for this service), or you could use your own diagrams (either computer generated or hand drawn—whatever you're most comfortable with). If you pay a contractor for this service, you shouldn't feel obligated to have them do the actual work. Specifications are the details—a list of products and materials to be used in the project that can include brand names, model numbers, and even colours.

Now use the plans and specifications to get contractor bids.

As you compare bids, look for value and quality, not just price. Think about what each contractor will bring to the job, especially in terms of the workmanship you saw or heard about when you checked out their references. And keep in mind that the contractor with the lowest price might not understand the job, or may be underestimating the time it will take.

Finally, go with your gut. Ask yourself how you feel about each contractor. Do you feel confident about them? Will you be able to communicate with them comfortably? You're going to be working with this person for a while, so personality matters. But don't fall for the smoothest talker. Pay attention to what the contractor's actually saying.

Detailed drawings and specifications allow contractors to make bids you can really compare

Now get it in writing!

I know what you're thinking: more details on paper before the work can even begin. It can feel like this part of the process takes forever. But a contract is your blueprint for how and when the work is expected to be done, and what it will cost, including how to deal with unforeseen delays or costs. Taking the time to get this part right will help you avoid sticky situations (or even legal messes) in the future.

At its most basic, the contract needs to cover two types of information:

1. Every aspect of the project you and the contractor have agreed to, including work to be done, material and product specifications, responsibility for building permits and inspections, the work schedule, price and payment arrangements, and the process for making change orders (you'll see more on change orders in the next section). The payment schedule should always be built around project benchmarks, not arbitrary dates on the calendar. Remember that at the end of the day the homeowner is always on the hook—legally—for getting the permits, even if you've decided the contractor will get them for you.

2. Proof that the contractor is operating their business properly, so you're protected from risks. This includes proof of business liability insurance, Workers' Compensation coverage or equivalent accidental injury insurance, proof of bonding and/or licensing where the government requires it, and proof of proper business registration (a business or GST/HST number).

Managing "extras"

If you stop and put your imagination to work on other things that might come up on the job, you can probably predict a few other items that need to be in your contract.

The first is a hot-button topic for contractors and homeowners alike: "extras." These are things that are added to the original agreement and that can end up taking a lot more time, and costing more, than you planned.

Most pros have a pretty good idea of what's behind the walls just because of the age of the building, but they may not be able to predict the condition of what they'll find,

Planning carefully from the beginning, including deciding on bathroom fixtures, will help avoid surprises and delays during your renovation.

or how much will be required to fix or work around it. When the walls of your house are opened up during the reno, your contractor will sometimes find things they weren't expecting—old knob-and-tube wiring, for example, in a house that's already had substantial work done on it in recent years, including supposedly "updated" electrical.

So how do you manage extras with your contractor? Your guiding principle should be fairness. What's fair? Whose choice—or mistake—caused the extra? Did you change your mind about something after the contract was signed and the bid accepted? Should the contractor—the professional and the expert in this relationship—have predicted the extra and included it into the fixed price?

Here's an example that happened on one of my projects: we pulled up the floor tile of a bad kitchen renovation and discovered a bare wire buried in the mortar. We looked further and discovered hidden junction boxes, hot wires dead-ended in walls, and dozens of other code violations waiting to burn down the house.

There was no way we could have anticipated wiring so bad, and no way we could leave it as it was. If your contractor finds a situation like that, it's fair to charge an extra to the contract to fix it. Of course, they'll have to explain it to you and have you sign off on the extra work and cost—before they start to work, not after.

Before the work starts, a good contractor will have given you a list detailing the decisions you have to make to keep the project on time and on budget. Bathroom fixtures, cabinets, stairs, doors, and windows all have lead times, and if you don't get your first choice in time to meet the work schedule, there's a chance you could be charged for delays or corrections to accommodate you. Delays cost money as well as time, and sometimes you need to pay a premium to rush orders so you can avoid further delays.

Your contractor can't read your mind, so if you make changes that are clearly not part of the original contract, you should expect to pay for them. If you change your mind on the colour of the paint, or the cupboards, or the style of countertop, what's fair then hinges on the cost of materials and how those changes affect the work schedule. Changes to the work schedule cost your contractor extra time and money—beyond the initial contract price.

There are two ways that these extra costs can be handled.

One way is to set aside a contingency budget in the contract. A contingency budget allows you and the contractor to resolve specific details as the work progresses. If unexpected costs arise, you'll have the funds to amend the contract accordingly.

Another way is to allow for change orders along the way, as needed. A change order is an amendment to your contract. When a hidden deficiency is discovered, or you, the homeowner, change your mind about something and deviate from the original work plan, the contractor will write up a summary of the costs involved and the extra time it will take. Once you've approved the summary, and you've both signed it, it becomes part of the contract—in fact, it's as legally binding as the contract itself.

Unscrupulous contractors will enter a low initial bid and then pounce on extras as a way of increasing their margins. If you get a price that is substantially lower than the others and you go for it, watch out for pricey extras. And by the same token, don't think you can hire a contractor for a fixed price, and then expect them to "throw it in" every time you change your mind or there's an unpredicted (and unpredictable) surprise.

Good planning from the beginning will reduce the number of extras you'll have, and the best way to control your costs is to keep extras down. A good contractor will handle extras properly by including a fair pricing procedure for them in the original contract. They'll charge in one of two ways—time and material or fixed price. Whenever possible, go with a fixed-price approach. And make sure that extras cannot proceed without a written and signed change order from you. Pros know how long something (without changes or surprises) is likely to take.

MIKE'S TIP

Custom costs

I've seen it happen often enough. The homeowner starts out with a modest plan for a kitchen or bathroom, a plan that includes stock cabinetry and laminate countertops. But as the work progresses, the homeowner sees the kitchen demolished, it's become a blank slate, and they're still looking around at all the great products out there, still dreaming about what their kitchen could look like. They start to think, "We've gone this far, why not go the whole way?" Suddenly they're asking for custom cabinets and granite countertops.

That's no problem, as long as you're willing to pay—and wait longer than originally planned, maybe even several months longer. It takes time for custom work to be measured, designed, and built, and in the case of granite or other natural stone countertops, the material sometimes has to be shipped in from the other side of the world, so you're looking at longer wait times.

Together with your general contractor, you'll write up a change order that details exactly what you want done, how much more time it will take, and what the cost will be. Also, with high-priced custom work, it's often expected that you'll pay the contractor up front for the cost of the custom work.

Contracts are worth the hassle

No one likes the process of coming up with a thorough, detailed contract. But let me be crystal clear about this: avoid the temptation to bypass this important step. The two things you really should not do are "seal the deal" with a handshake only, or worse, "go underground" by agreeing to a cash-only arrangement.

The first situation is obviously a bad idea: if a disagreement arises, you've got nothing in writing to support your position.

The second situation is even worse. It's risky because the cash market doesn't protect you from risks related to poor work or dishonesty by the contractor, and it could leave you liable for thousands (or even millions) if someone gets injured on the job.

You might also think that by hiring a contractor for cash, you don't have anything to worry about. After all, it's the contractor who's breaking the law, right? Well, yes and no. If a contractor isn't reporting income and paying taxes, they won't want their name turning up on other government records like Workers' Compensation files, business license applications, or building permits.

So where would that leave you?

For one thing, it would leave you without a building permit—which you need for almost any residential renovation. It's the property owner, not the contractor, who is legally responsible for meeting building code and permit requirements. If a permit is

Custom cabinetry, natural stone counters and tile, as well as multiple shower heads—great finishes, but best included in your contract, not as extras.

required, and a municipal building inspector finds out you didn't get one, they can put a stop to the work until a permit is in place, or even order the work torn down at your expense.

That's just one example. There are a number of other laws that can affect you if you hire underground—things like Workers' Compensation, consumer protection against overcharging, security of deposits, and construction liens. New-home warranty programs won't apply if you're having a renovation done. Without a legal, above-board working relationship with your contractor, where will you turn if something goes wrong?

Construction work involves risks. When someone works on your home, you need to be protected. Just because the job is simple or small doesn't mean something can't go wrong.

When it comes to contracts, there are just a few basic principles to follow: Work with pros. Stay legitimate. And put everything in writing.

As I've said again and again, hiring right is probably the most important decision you'll make during a renovation. Get the right person for the job, and put together a contract that spells out everything you can think of. Remember that the point of the contract isn't to create some weapon you can use in court. The point of the contract is to ensure everyone is clear on what the project is, what the schedule is, and how to get the job done successfully.

Once the contract is in place, always make sure that you're fulfilling your part of the agreement, especially in terms of payments and scheduling. Be the best client you can be, and you might be surprised at how much more you'll enjoy the process.

A contract and conduct checklist

Before you sign the contract:

❑ **Check the contractor's references.**

❑ **Know exactly what you want.**

- ❏ **Iron out every detail of cost, scheduling and design, as well as managing extras.**
- ❏ **Have a realistic budget, and set a payment schedule in the written contract.**
- ❏ **Do your homework so you understand the job almost as well as the contractor does.**

Once the work has begun:
- ❏ **Start a job log.**
- ❏ **Conduct regular meetings.**
- ❏ **Bring up concerns immediately and respectfully to your contractor only and not the trades (electricians, plumbers, etc.).**
- ❏ **Take photos before, during, and after.**
- ❏ **Never relax your expectations.**
- ❏ **Fulfill your part of the agreement.**
- ❏ **If you must make changes, detail them in a change order.**

Workplace safety: How you can help

Not too long ago, one of my crew members lost a family member in a workplace accident. It was a terrible tragedy that this young man lost his life, and that loss will affect his family, friends, and co-workers forever. For me it was a reminder that all of us need to work safely, and that you as a homeowner also need to make sure your contractor is working safely.

It's shocking to me that on average, five workers die in Canada every workday on job sites, and many more are injured in falls or workplace accidents. Every work site has potential hazards: chemicals, heavy equipment, and power tools, for example. Workers can get heat stroke from high temperatures or frostbite from the cold. They can slip, trip, or fall from a height.

I'm not saying that you, as the homeowner, have to be on-site as the safety officer, but you should be aware of the basics. And those basics start when you hire your contractor. Ask the right questions and you can play a role in reducing injuries on the job.

Ask your contractor about their health and safety record. Ask for proof of Workers' Compensation coverage. Ask if they have any safety training, and what their health and safety practices are. Ask if the contractor will make sure the workers wear and use personal protective equipment (PPE). That means hard hats and CSA-approved safety boots, eye and ear protection, work gloves, fall-arrest gear if they're working at a height above 3 metres, dust masks, and respirators.

Check that the contractor will have a properly stocked first-aid kit on-site at all times. That kit should include bandages, ointments, dressings, gauze, cold compresses, burn treatments, emergency eye care, and pain-relief products.

Once your contractor has begun the job, make sure they're keeping safety in mind. Is the job site clean? My biggest pet peeve is a dirty job site—if the floors are slippery from sawdust, and construction debris is scattered around, it's a recipe for disaster. I've told the story of when I was working with my dad and how he kept on telling me to clean up, and I said I'd get around to it. I put up a ladder over a hole in the floor that was covered in debris—down I went. Nothing was hurt but my dignity. But it could have been much worse.

Clean-up is a big part of the job. Garbage and scrap has to be constantly picked up and put into bins and dumpsters and kept away from walkways, stairs, and other traffic paths. Or, if there's no bin, make sure the contractor is piling garbage and scrap into a single, out-of-the-way spot.

If the workers are on your roof or on the edge of an upper floor, they should be protected by a sturdy guardrail or be wearing proper fall-arrest equipment—a safety belt or harness—that's been properly secured.

Is your contractor excavating around your foundation? Is the trench properly sloped back to prevent collapse or cave-in? Or is it properly supported by a shoring system?

Are there young workers or apprentices on the job? If so, that's great—I respect contractors who take on apprentices and help them get their training and hours. But are those young people working without direct supervision? I hope not—and I've seen more than a few bad renovations that were sold by the contractor, who then left the young, inexperienced labourers to do the job—badly, and sometimes dangerously.

MIKE'S TIP

A growing need

Canada has a shortage of skilled trades and it's only getting bigger. I'm doing what I can to encourage young people to pursue a career in the trades, but it may take you longer than you expect to hire right. Don't get frustrated and bail on this important step. It can take longer to hire right than to do your renovation.

A clean job site is a sign of a good contractor. Messy sites can be unsafe and can be a red flag that you've hired the wrong contractor.

It's a fact that when demand is high for contractors there's more bad work being done. That's because there are only so many good, experienced contractors available, and many homeowners who are anxious to get started on their home renovation just won't wait. They'd rather take a chance and play the slot machine of bad contractors. And when the economy heats up and more workers flood into an industry to find work, injuries rise. The new guys sometimes get inadequate safety training, and everyone's rushing and careless. It's a bad combination: inexperienced workers, potentially dangerous workplaces, and no safety equipment or training.

Your home, while it's under renovation, is considered a workplace. If an injury occurs due to unsafe practices, it's possible that you could also be charged and fined, and your job site shut down.

Your renovation project needs to be protected against delay and additional cost. You need to be protected against liability. But most importantly, the crew working on your house needs to be protected against injury. Make sure your contractor works safely.

Should you kick your contractor off the job?

I often hear from renovating homeowners who are fed up with their contractor and want to kick them off the site. Usually by then the situation is so bad and the anger and frustration so overwhelming that I can't believe there was ever a civilized word between them. So my first thought is, "How did you let it get this bad?"

Before you start yelling, check your contract. Read it again before you do anything. Look for what lawyers call "the limitations of liability" that are imposed on the contractor: the timetable, the types of materials used, the pricing for extras. Then look at the situation you're in as objectively as you can and ask, "Has the contractor actually violated any of the limitations?"

Ask yourself if it's a substantial violation. It's a big deal to kick your contractor off the job. You can't do that for a minor mistake like painting a wall the wrong colour. It better be for something a lot bigger, like not complying with building or safety bylaws, being significantly late on the schedule compared to the original plan, or billing more than agreed for an extra—without an acceptable explanation.

Don't be surprised if you find out that—no matter how angry you are—your contractor hasn't broken the agreement. And don't be surprised that even if it appears they have broken the agreement, your case against them isn't as black and white as you believe.

Here's an example of what often happens: You discover the contract requires the contractor or their representative to be working on-site at least three days a week and you haven't seen either of them for two weeks. Got him, you think! But then you read the rest of the contract, which allows your contractor an exception if they can claim there have been delays as a result of changes you made to the scope of work that have disrupted the schedule. You did make changes, didn't you? And the contractor did say they would disrupt the schedule, right? Well, whose fault is it then? And are you justified in kicking your contractor off the job?

Let's say you really have found something substantial. The contract will have something to say about how you're allowed to respond. Usually, contracts will require you to notify your contractor of your objection in writing and then give them time to make it right. You have to follow the instructions laid out in the contract before you can do anything drastic.

So start sending your notifications, and do two other things:

1. Have a job log where you can record the offences.

2. Bring in another contractor or quantity surveyor as a third party who can make your case from an expert's point of view. I have to say you should have started the log from the beginning of the job, especially if you're dealing with a bunch of little violations over time, but it's never too late to start.

With that, you're all set to give notice to the contractor. But don't expect it to be over. In fact it's just beginning, and what you now have on your hands is potentially years of court hearings and lawyer's fees, which gets me back to my first question: How did this happen? What did you do to let it get this bad? Being in this situation is like the guy nailing plywood over his windows in the middle of the hurricane. There's always, always plenty of warning. What were you so busy doing that you didn't see the clouds on the horizon?

Remember, we're not talking about fraudulent activity. This is two people starting on a project with good intentions in good faith and with a clear understanding of what's involved.

Or was it? Were your intentions good? Did you hire the contractor with the lowest price knowing they weren't going to get the necessary permits? Did you act in good faith? Were you already thinking you could beat the holdback out of the contractor if you complained enough when the project was done? Did you completely understand what was involved, or did you just stop listening and hope nothing bad would happen when the contractor said there could be complications once they started digging?

Don't find yourself trying to cover your windows in a hurricane. Look at the horizon and read the weather forecast.

The final walk-through

It's easy to be exhausted at the end of a renovation—especially a long one. You just want it to be over so you can move back in and move on with your lives.

When your renovation is complete, walk through it carefully and detail any outstanding work that may need to be done. Take your time and take photos if you need to.

But no matter what, you still need to go through and list everything that isn't completely satisfactory. This list becomes the centrepiece for getting the job finished like it should be. You will identify incomplete work or work that's been done improperly, oversights by your contractor, or defects in the materials.

Don't forget—your contractor is moving on too. They have other jobs to go on to and won't like being called back for each little fix-up you come across in the weeks ahead. They need to wrap up your job so they can move on to the next—they've got to make a living, after all. Do it efficiently—make a list.

Many people feel uncomfortable about going over deficiencies with their contractor—they may have established a sort of friendship with the contractor and feel awkward "forcing" them to fix things they aren't satisfied with—or worse, withholding payment until those things are fixed.

Don't. Your contractor won't be surprised to find you aren't willing to make the final payment on the contract until everything is satisfactory—that only makes sense to a professional.

At the close of a renovation, the contractor should call you (and your architect or representative and anyone else who has a stake in the success of the project) for a walk-through to identify anything that remains to be done, isn't up to standard, or has some defect that needs attention. If the contractor doesn't call you to set this up, by all means take the initiative and set up the meeting yourself!

Your contractor should have the latest set of plans with them and a long checklist of things to look at. This walk-through is your chance to bring up anything that concerns you. You're looking for flaws in the paint or drywall, odd-looking spots on the ceiling where the stucco is badly done—anything that doesn't look right. You'll look at the transition between the old and the new work. You'll test whether the doors open and close properly. You'll be trying all the taps, filling the tub with water, and running the dishwasher and using the kitchen sink. The furnace should be turned up (or the air conditioning in the summer) so you can hear it running. Listen to how the ductwork responds to the load, and feel the air blowing from the registers. Look at the joints in the baseboard trim, the corners where the walls meet, and the cleanliness of the ceramic tile surfaces.

Check behind things. Stick your head in the kitchen cabinets and run your hand over the back of the cabinet doors. Is the finish to the standard you were told to expect? Trace the plumbing pipes as far as you can in the basement and satisfy yourself the installation is neat and clean.

Pull and push things. See if you can lift the countertops. Jump on the floors to check for flex or soft spots. Press on the ceramic backsplash in various places. See if you can rattle the doors when they're closed. Grab the window frame and give it a tug.

If you're starting to think the walk-through might take a while, you're right. Depending on the size of the project, you should expect to spend between four hours and a full day doing it. The goal is to subject all the installations to normal use to see how they stand up. However, if you've been doing your job as a homeowner, you're already familiar with the guts of the job—that is, everything under the surface. At this point, your inspection should mainly be about cosmetics.

Ask lots and lots of questions. If you have an architect involved, lean on their expertise to help you understand what you're seeing. If you don't, you should consider having a third-party expert (a home inspector, or another contractor hired as a consultant) to be your advocate. As you go through the house, the contractor should be making notes, marking up the plans, and filling out their checklist where there are issues, but you should be making your own notes too. A tape recorder might be handy for you to help remember what you talked about.

If the list of deficiencies is long, give the contractor a couple of weeks to clean them up and try again. Whatever you do, don't rush. Make sure you're happy. It's your best chance to make sure the work done is done right.

Don't make that final payment to your contractor until you're 100% satisfied with the work, and until the contractor has provided you with a final invoice showing the amount has been paid in full. It goes like this: invoice first, then inspection, then satisfaction, and then final payment released (this is not the holdback). If this process continues too long, it might be wise to put the money in trust to show that it's actually there, and that you aren't just stalling for time because you're broke.

"Substantially complete"? Now hold back 10%

I've mentioned the importance of having a holdback clause in your contract from the outset. The holdback is the last 10% of the total value of the contract you "hold back" from the contractor after the job has been substantially completed. Most homeowners think the holdback exists to make sure the contractor comes back to finish the job. They're wrong.

The holdback exists to protect you from liens—by the contractor, the subtrades, or suppliers—against your property. Most provinces across Canada provide contract law which says you have 45 days to pay the last 10% of the contract price on your renovation once you agree the work is substantially done.

Your contractor—or the subtrades—have 45 days from substantial completion of your job to file a claim of lien against your property. You need to wait that 45 days for the time limit to expire before you fully pay out your contractor.

The holdback is not your insurance that things will be done right—the payment schedule is. I always tell people to build the payment schedule on their job around benchmarks. Once the contractor reaches a certain stage of completion, you release more money.

If you're unhappy with the way the job is progressing, stop paying the general contractor until things get back on track. It doesn't matter what kind of contract you have, whether it's a fixed price, or time and materials, or a project management contract. If the contractor isn't performing up to their standards, or more importantly, your standards, hold back any further money until you can rectify the situation.

The holdback clause, on the other hand, is designed to protect the subtrades who do the work and then don't get paid. It's to make sure they aren't ripped off by the contractor for the work they've done.

Sometimes a contractor will satisfy the terms of the contract, and the homeowners are happy with the finished job. But the contractor will "forget" to pay the subtrades, and they're left holding the bag. Their only recourse is to lien the house—your house—in an attempt to get paid by the homeowners what they're owed. And a subtrade or supplier who hasn't been paid has the right to put a lien on your property for 45 days after the job is substantially completed.

No, it's not fair. But your house is where they've invested their labour and materials. They have a stake in it.

If a lien is filed against your property, you can't sell that property until the lien has been paid or discharged. It's a legal claim against the value of your home. If you've paid the entire contract amount to the contractor, but a lien is filed, you're still required to pay the liens out of your pocket. Having money held back allows you to clear the lien with the money that you set aside for the original contract.

"Substantial completion"

Once you agree with the contractor that the job is substantially done, meaning 97% of the job is complete, you may be asked to sign a certificate of substantial completion. It's at this point that you have to choose to sign or not to sign, to agree or not to agree, based on how happy you are with the work. If you're not happy, you don't sign.

Many customers feel intimidated determining substantial completion, even if the contractor is being perfectly professional. It's normal to feel pressure to get everything over with as the job nears its end. But if you bring up your concerns as they come up during the renovation, there won't be any surprises for you or your contractor at the end.

Until the time limit for filing a lien has passed, make sure you hold back the final payment. The law says you have 45 days, so make sure you take them—no matter how much you like your contractor, no matter how happy you are with the renovation, no matter how much you believe the contractor will be back to finish the job.

Take that 45 days to make sure the job is done, that you're satisfied with the work, and that the subtrades have all been paid by the contractor.

Your end of the bargain: How to be a great client

I get many e-mails from frustrated people who tell me that they've had all kinds of contractors look at their job and then never even quote on the project. In the end, the person they decide to hire isn't their first choice, or even their second or third choice, but the one—the only one—who agreed to take the job. It's a frustrating start to what will likely be a lousy renovation.

So why does this happen? Wouldn't you think a contractor wants to work, that they want to take on your renovation job? This is going to sound harsh, but maybe it's not them. Maybe it's you. Maybe your job isn't a good one, and there are lots of possible reasons for that.

Homeowners need to understand that good contractors want to make sure the job is right for them, too. For good contractors—the ones with the right attitude and the ones that take pride in their work—this job is also about their next job. Good contractors know they're really only as good as their last project. Their reputation matters and referrals from satisfied clients are important.

Keep this in mind: the next time a contractor comes to look at your renovation, they're looking at what you want and need, and whether they can successfully deliver it given your budget, expectations, and timelines, and who else is working on the job. If they feel they might have to compromise their standards of quality—let's say your budget expectations are too low or you want the job rushed or you've hired some subtrades who aren't skilled—they'll walk away from your job.

This is a great time to be honest with your contractor. As much as you need to make a good decision, let your contractor have as much information as possible. Let them know your honest expectations and help them to help you—maybe what you're thinking about isn't realistic within your budget. A good contractor will let you know that, and if you aren't open to hearing so, they'll walk away. A bad contractor will promise to give you what you ask for, even if it's impossible.

Remember the contractor has to deal with suppliers, inspectors, engineers, and subtrades every day. That's the world your contractor lives in. They can't afford to damage those relationships for a project that they can see, going into it, is unrealistic.

I hear good contractors refer to their work as "my plumbing" or "my wiring" or "my roofing"—it shows they take pride in the work they do. They feel a sense of ownership and responsibility for the project. And they won't commit to a job that they know will be a problem, that they won't be able to feel proud of, and that might end up badly.

The homeowner and a good contractor are both looking for the same basic thing—a good job. The homeowner wants to look at their completed renovation and know they got value for their time and efforts, and take pride in the results. So does the contractor.

Be honest with prospective contractors about your expectations, and be realistic about how much it's going to cost, and you're more likely to find the good contractors lining up to work for you, instead of having to chase them down.

Questions to ask contractors

You want your prospective contractor to ask a lot of questions, but you need to ask a lot too, so that you avoid the nightmare of hiring the wrong contractor. Ask these questions and more:

1. **How long have you been working as a contractor?**
2. **Do you specialize in one area?**
3. **Who looks after getting permits?**
4. **How many jobs does your company have in progress right now?**
5. **Who will be on-site and in charge of my job each day?**
6. **Do you have a portfolio that shows insurance, certifications, a licence, and photos of the work you've done?**
7. **Who will be doing the electrical, plumbing, and insulation on the project?**
8. **Do you have a list of references?**

Questions to ask references

Don't skip this step. Call your contractor's references—all of them—and ask lots of questions. Better yet, go see the contractor's work. Some questions to start with:

1. **Did the contractor start and finish on time?**
2. **Did the contractor charge you money at the end of the job that you didn't expect?**
3. **Was the contractor courteous and clean?**
4. **Did the contractor keep you involved in the project by explaining what they were doing or telling you when something unexpected happened?**
5. **Did the contractor get permits?**
6. **Can I visit your home to see the work the contractor completed?**

CHAPTER 4

Greening
Your Renovation

More and more homeowners want their renovation to be as green as it can be, and I think that's great. It's also the right thing to do. When you're working on a kitchen or bathroom, there are a lot of green options to choose from. But it's important to understand there are different shades of green—and decide for yourself if you want to be light or dark green.

Different products use the word "green" as part of their marketing strategy, and in truth a lot of it is crap. A lot of that stuff isn't "green" at all. When we use green products in our building we want to make sure we go "dark green"—which means understanding what's really "green."

What's Really "Green"?

Green building is about systems and integration. You need to think about the whole life of the project. If a building material you'd like to use isn't biological—that means it completely biodegrades and decomposes without affecting the natural environment—then it should be a non-toxic and non-harmful synthetic that lasts a long time and has no negative effects on the environment.

That's a lot to ask of a product, and a lot to expect a homeowner to learn. How much is the average homeowner supposed to understand? Isn't it tough enough managing your renovation, finding a good contractor, and keeping your project on track? It comes down to how committed you are to the environment.

Who's going to pay for it?

Many green home construction features have a higher upfront cost than standard products, but you'll often save money in the long run because you'll be buying better quality, and will have a more energy-efficient home in the end.

People who are into renovations for a quick buck won't be the ones to invest in some green technology that will take years to pay back. Just one more reason among many why I've never been a fan of the idea of flipping houses for profit. I think people should invest in their house and make it their home. In fact, I think one of the problems with new houses today is that people buy them without planning on staying there. If we did, the houses would be built differently; they'd be built to last. Odds are that every renovation puts some more material into a landfill somewhere. Just one more reason to make sure that your reno lasts.

What makes it green?

Saying something is "natural" doesn't necessarily make it good. Asbestos is natural. So is mould. It's a good idea to look for third-party certifications—EcoLogo, Green Seal, and Green Label are great—because you know the product has been tested and has passed.

There are lots of reasons a product can be called green. For instance:

- **It's made of recycled or salvaged material.**
- **It uses environmentally safe and health-safe materials.**
- **It lasts a very long time and won't need to be replaced soon.**
- **It's made with a rapidly renewable resource that can be harvested frequently (such as straw bales or bamboo).**
- **It has low or no emission of toxic chemicals into the air (see more on low-VOC products on page 88).**
- **No toxins result from its manufacture.**
- **It saves energy and water.**
- **It uses renewable energy.**
- **It can be recycled at the end of its useful life.**
- **The cost of transportation is low (made locally, lightweight, can be built on location).**

But there are other questions to ask yourself: How is the material grown, harvested, processed, shipped, and transported? Some products are green, but are they green across their entire lifecycle? For example, some woods claim to be green for flooring because wood is a renewable resource. But maybe that fact is offset a lot by improper forestry techniques and the long distances that wood has to travel to find its market.

MIKE'S TIP

Green wood

One of the easiest ways to help green your renovation is by choosing the right lumber. FSC-certified wood is not hard to find; it's in big box stores too. Forestry practices are monitored by the Forestry Stewardship Council (FSC). Engineered wood, one of my favourite products, is made from fast-growing "weed" trees and compressed under high pressure. The wood is strong and solid—great for structural beams.

One of the greenest woods is actually blue. BluWood is coated to protect against moisture and insects, so it's a good choice where these are issues.

Whatever you choose, good contractors plan carefully and pay attention to lumber dimensions so they only order as much wood as they need to minimize waste. And that's thinking green.

Green choices on their own may not be that green. A house made of 100% wood—a log cabin, for instance—would be very green, since it's all organic. But wood isn't a great insulator and that house will lose a lot of heat in winter. It's not energy efficient, so how green is it?

Recycled?

Some products are recycled and recyclable. That's a great selling feature, but maybe it's not such a great product in the end—maybe it won't last long. Maybe it's only partly recycled.

Does it use post-consumer or post-industrial materials in its manufacture? It's greener if the recycled material is post-consumer waste, instead of post-industrial waste, since consumer waste is more likely to end up in a landfill.

The bottom line is that you have to read the fine print and check out the facts before accepting the "recycled" label as fact.

How green are you?

As I said, there are shades of green. Some people are committed to being energy-efficient and resource-efficient and building with locally available, sustainably harvested, renewable resources that are non-toxic. That's the greenest you can be.

Other homeowners may decide to build with conventional materials but finish with natural fibre carpets, energy efficient appliances, and low-VOC paints.

As you plan the detail of your kitchen or bathroom renovation, you need to determine how committed you are to being environmentally responsible during every phase of your project, including the initial tear-down.

Green demolition: The three Rs at work

Any renovation project will create waste, and that can be a huge problem. Canada produces more solid waste per capita than many other countries, and waste from construction, renovation, and demolition accounts for about one-third of that waste. Talk about stress on the environment.

If you and your contractor agree to incorporate the three Rs (reduce, reuse, and recycle) into your reno project, you're making a significant contribution to the environment. You'll reduce the waste that goes to landfill sites. And by finding ways to reuse or recycle materials, you'll help to reduce the need to extract more raw materials for building.

What can you do?

First of all, plan for waste management. Find out where various materials can be reused or recycled, and make arrangements for pickup or drop-off in advance of your demolition. Some items will need to be stored on-site as you work, so make sure you have bins or other storage containers planned for these.

MIKE'S TIP

Making use of salvage

Check your local re-use centres, like the Habitat for Humanity's ReStore, for things that you might be able to use in your reno. Sometimes these centres also get surplus overstock, factory overruns, and excess inventory or end-of-line products from manufacturers that you can buy for a fraction of the regular retail price.

There are a lot of advantages to reusing old building materials. For one thing, the purchase price will be lower than buying new off the shelf or custom. There's the environmental savings we all get from recycling. And sometimes older, weathered-and-worn materials can give a renovation project a special look that you can't get with new fixtures and materials.

You need to be aware of the real differences between surplus new, used, and antique before you start shopping, though. For instance, antique windows with single panes of glass won't have much thermal value, so they're probably not a sensible idea. You might use them as a decorative element, but not in place of energy-efficient windows. A better idea if you're looking to save on windows would be to search the re-use centre for surplus new models that might be perfect for your renovation needs.

In the case of salvaged wood, you may have better luck. A lot of wood used in old buildings was large, first-growth timber of a quality that is just not available now. It can be very stable, with few knots, and comes in larger dimensions than anything being sold today. The patina of age can add beauty to wood and add character to a project's look, whether it's flooring, cabinetry, wall panelling, or even furniture. You may not be able to use salvaged lumber for anything structural, but I bet you'd have a hard time matching the beauty of salvaged wood mouldings or a fireplace mantel, no matter how much time and money you spent.

It's important to understand that not everything can be reused. For example, lead paint can make an old piece of timber a health liability. If you find old lighting fixtures, you'll have to take them to a professional electrician to make sure they're safe to use and wired up to current code.

What can be reused?

Building materials in good condition can often be reused. Examples are acoustical ceiling tiles, doors, light fixtures, and cabinetry.

There are many companies that deal in used building materials. Look in the Yellow Pages under "Building Materials, Used" to find companies that will pick up your salvage, or contact one of the fifty-eight cross-Canada locations of the Habitat for Humanity ReStore. It's not hard to find someone who will take your used building materials off your hands. One person's trash is another's treasure.

What can be recycled?

Some items can't be reused, but they can be recycled. Scrap metal (including old wiring) is a prime candidate for recycling, and there are many metal recyclers across the country, in almost every major centre. Wood waste, drywall, asphalt shingles, concrete, and carpeting are all recyclable as well. Even the earth you pull from the ground for a foundation can be hauled away, as long as it's clean fill.

There are also a growing number of "mixed" recycling operations for construction, renovation, and demolition waste. These outlets will allow contractors to place different kinds of waste in a single waste collection bin, which reduces space and labour requirements on-site. There's a charge (usually per tonne) for handling waste in this way, however.

What's it going to cost?

There's a cost to getting rid of real waste—the stuff that's left over after you've recycled—at a landfill. The more you can divert through recycling or reusing, the

Much of the waste from a renovation can be recycled, including drywall and metal, so it's worth separating it from landfill.

less you will spend on landfill fees. Yes, it will probably mean more time on the job site to take the room apart carefully rather than tearing it out, but some research shows that the added labour costs are offset by the reduction in fees combined with the money you'll make from selling used materials such as metal for recycling.

At the beginning of the job is a good time to ask a prospective contractor how they plan to handle the waste from your job site. It's another way to see if your contractor's principles and style match yours.

Green design

Green design includes many things. For example:

- **greater energy efficiency (programmable thermostats, increased insulation, a better-constructed building envelope, energy-efficient windows and doors)**
- **improved indoor air quality (hardwood or tile instead of carpet, no- or low-VOC materials, high-efficiency furnaces)**
- **water conservation (recycling rainwater for landscape irrigation/ car washing to reduce load on sewer system; low-flow showers and toilets).**

When building a new home, using the site effectively is important. Good site planning can reduce the amount of energy a home needs. Strategically placed windows can provide passive solar heat in winter, and give you enough ventilation to reduce or even eliminate the need for air conditioning in the hot months of the year. Sometimes the windows you add during a renovation can help you get closer to this goal, too.

The first step to increase energy efficiency is to add or improve insulation, caulking, and weatherstripping wherever possible. Next on your list should be double-glazed/Low-E windows and high-efficiency appliances. The money you spend on better insulation and windows will start saving you money right away on heating and cooling bills.

Other energy upgrades include installing solar water preheaters, photovoltaic panels, or getting "green power" generated from renewable sources like the sun, wind, and geothermal energy (the earth itself).

All about volatile organic compounds

If you want a green renovation, you need to make sure the products you use are low-VOC (volatile organic compounds). VOCs are basically chemicals, such as formaldehyde, that are by-products of many building supplies and products. They evaporate quickly into your indoor air—that's why they're "volatile"—and can affect your air quality. They can cause dizziness and headaches, eye irritation, and asthmatic reactions—and at high concentrations they can be toxic. Millions of people are chemically sensitive, and even low levels of VOCs can make them really sick.

VOCs are emitted from all kinds of products you'll use in a renovation—treated wood products, insulation, adhesives, carpets and other types of flooring, paint, cabinets, and furniture. VOCs are also an issue with products used on the exterior, with asphalt shingles being a great example. On one roof, the off-gassing of petrochemicals might not mean much, but when you multiply that by thousands or even hundreds of thousands of roofs, it's obviously a problem. Steel is a better choice for the environment, and it performs better too.

Newly constructed homes that have just been renovated have higher-than-normal levels of VOCs. Those levels decrease over time as the VOCs evaporate into the air and the air is dispersed. Some products—like spray foam insulation—will cure quickly, and within a few days the VOCs are virtually gone or are at non-detectable levels. Other products—like pressed-wood cabinets—will off-gas for much longer. And if the material is exposed to high temperatures or high moisture levels, the level of emission will be higher.

If you're considering wood floors, reclaimed wood is an obvious green choice.

Make better choices

You need to talk to your contractor and do your homework so you can make informed decisions about indoor air quality when you select materials to use in your home. You need to find out what the product is made of and whether it off-gasses. The truth is many building products—especially man-made ones—do. Glass, ceramic tile, metal, stone, and other hard and inert materials don't release any VOCs.

Kitchen cabinets are usually made of medium-density fibreboard, plywood, or particle board that contain glues high in formaldehyde. And they often have a sprayed-on finish that will off-gas for many months. Choosing solid wood over composite wood products that contain formaldehyde is a good idea. Consider tile, hardwood, or linoleum instead of vinyl flooring, or natural carpet instead of a synthetic. If you can afford it, go for custom solid wood cabinetry with a low- or zero-VOC finish.

All engineered and manufactured wood products are made with at least some adhesives and resins, and most of those will off-gas. That includes plywood, oriented strand board, laminated beams, medium-density fibreboard, and particleboard. If these building materials are used in the framing and structure of the house, they'll be separated from the living space by drywall and plaster, which will help to some degree with off-gassing. The environmental upside of engineered lumber is that it's manufactured from "weed trees" (ash and poplar) that are fast-growing and easily replaceable, and the amount of glue used is quite small.

Paints and adhesives

Most paints contain VOCs because paints are formulated with solvents to improve their application or durability. But now you can find low- or no-VOC paints that have almost no odours as they cure. Be aware that the base paint might be low-VOC, but the tints that are added for colour might not be.

Water-based paints and adhesives have lower levels of VOCs than solvent-based products. And cleaning the brushes and equipment you use with oil-based paints involves using even more solvents, which go directly into the water supply, so water-based is the way to go.

How low is it?

You need to be careful when buying products and materials that say they're low VOC. The label might make that claim, but like calling a product "green" or "natural," it could mean anything. "Low VOC" from one company might just mean "lower than before," but it's still really high when compared with other similar products in the marketplace.

You need to buy products that have been tested and certified to emit low levels of VOCs. One standard to look for is the Green Seal. This says that a product has been rigorously evaluated and tested and meets certain standards that make it "environmentally preferable." In both Canada and the United States, the carpet manufacturing industry has created a Green Label to certify that certain carpets meet low-VOC requirements.

Following up: Checklist

Going green means figuring out where and when you're willing to choose the greenest options. Are you willing to sometimes pay extra, or work a little harder, to find the right products, in order to make environmentally friendly choices?

Your green priorities (check any that apply):

- ❏ products made of recycled or salvaged material
- ❏ products that use environmentally safe and healthy materials
- ❏ products that last a very long time and won't need to be replaced soon
- ❏ products made with a rapidly renewable resource that can be harvested frequently
- ❏ low-VOC (or no-VOC) products
- ❏ products that don't create toxins during manufacturing
- ❏ products that save energy and water
- ❏ products that use renewable energy

Green materials, fixtures, or appliances that you plan to use in your renovation:

If you're planning a green demolition:

Any items that can be salvaged:

_____

Any items that can be reused in your new kitchen or bathroom:

_____

Possible drop-off sites for salvage:

_____

Possible drop-off sites for safe hazardous waste disposal:

_____

CHAPTER 5

Cooking Up a Kitchen That Works

When you think about the design of your kitchen, you have to consider both looks and function—how it looks on the outside, and how it functions on the inside. You have to ask yourself a lot of questions as you make choices for your kitchen. For example, do you want to use wood or a synthetic product for the cabinets? Will you go with stock cabinets or spend much more on high-quality custom cabinets? What sort of colour scheme works best for you? What's the most efficient layout?

The questions I've just raised—along with many others—are what you should ask yourself as you design your new kitchen, either on your own or with the help of a professional designer. If you've done a realistic assessment of the space you've got to work with and the mechanical components that need to be addressed, you're already halfway there. There will be advantages and disadvantages to every space, because every kitchen is unique. But once you apply the rules of good kitchen design, you should end up with a kitchen that's efficient and safe—and it should look great.

A huge part of design is careful planning, and the rest is knowing the rules of good design. Yes, there are tried-and-true rules for how to make spaces work better and more efficiently. Just think about a restaurant kitchen, and imagine how much planning goes into one—everything has to be in the right place to make sure all those complicated meals can be prepared at the same time, at record speeds.

Even in a residential kitchen, efficiency matters. In fact, I'll bet one of the reasons you're thinking of redoing your kitchen is that you don't think it's efficient enough. Maybe you spend too much time walking between sink and stove. Maybe there never seems to be enough storage. Maybe you feel frustrated every time you try to cook because the counter space is too limited, or you're bumping into someone else. Whatever the problems might be right now, a kitchen reno is the time to correct them. Take the time to think carefully and plan for everything. Make notes about problems you find with your current kitchen design. They will usually have to do with not having enough space, or not having things where you need them.

In the kitchen, do you find there's never a place to put the groceries when you walk in the door loaded down with shopping bags? When you take a hot pot off the stove do you search for a place to set it because you don't have counter space on both sides of the cooktop? Do you find that you're always wishing for more storage room?

Write down the things that drive you crazy because they're exactly what will help you plan a better kitchen.

Coulda, woulda, shoulda:
Questions about your kitchen to ask from the start

Is there one thing you've always wanted to change about your kitchen?
Pay attention to this. You'll regret it if your new kitchen doesn't fix a problem you've noticed for years.

Is there one feature—such as wall ovens, an island with a prep sink in it, a spectacular built-in unit to house all your recyclables, or a computer nook— that would make your life easier in the kitchen?
If you've got a great idea, make it a priority to incorporate it into your final design.

Is there a high-end product or finish that always catches your eye when you look at magazines or books?
You probably can't afford to go with your first choice on every detail in the kitchen, but you might be able to splurge in one or two areas and satisfy your craving for luxury.

Are there features that you've always wanted?
From drawer dividers to dual-temperature wine storage units, there are thousands of great kitchen design ideas out there. Start a file with magazine clippings, or photocopies from books, of features you like. You can't incorporate every great idea, but you'll have a better chance of getting the ones you really want if you have a system to remember they're out there.

When planning your new kitchen, don't forget about in-cabinet hardware like pull-out shelves for awkward corner cabinets, and specialized storage hardware that can make your space more efficient.

How open should your kitchen be?

Be honest: Are you the spic-and-span kind of housekeeper whose kitchen can be on display any time at all, or is it a better idea to shield your guests from the disaster zone you create when you cook? What about your preferences: Do you like company while you work, or do you work best when you can concentrate on your own? Do you need to keep an eye on the kids while you're in the kitchen? Think about what a real day is like for you, and keep these considerations in mind as you plan.

You can build storage for books or wine into the end of an island.

Do you have collections that require special storage?

Cookbooks, vintage dishes, spices, a rolling pin collection—whatever. If you've got a lot of it, make sure you've got a place to store it. Don't let a standard design leave you without the room you need. Count and measure what you've got to make sure you allow enough space for it all—and leave some room for your collections to grow as well.

Is your kitchen a room with a view?

Maybe you want to capture even more of that view with a larger window, or possibly doors to the outside. The most desirable kitchens in today's real estate market have lots of sunlight and easy access to the outdoors. But don't interrupt the cook: always plan the kitchen so you're directing traffic around the work area rather than through it.

Can you bring more light into your kitchen?

More windows, bigger windows—you get a space that feels better, and more daylight means you can turn off lights and save on electricity.

What's your cooking fuel—electricity or gas? Do you plan to switch from one to the other during the reno?

If you need to bring in a gas line, or move it, make sure you budget for this. Maybe you'll go wild and even have a wood-burning pizza oven. Remember to plan for ventilation of fumes and moisture with direct venting to the outside.

Would your home work better if the kitchen had a larger eating area?

Sometimes all it takes to make a kitchen flow better is a bit more space for the table and chairs. If so, consider the possibility of a "bump-out" during your reno. That tiny "addition" could give you space and lots more light. Just make sure your contractor supports it structurally, and uses a closed-cell polyurethane foam insulation on the walls and floor to keep the cold out. And never let your contractor talk you into doing a project like this without getting all the necessary permits.

Do you need a professional designer?

It's no secret that I'm a believer in hiring the pros. In a kitchen overhaul, making design mistakes can cost you big money, so it makes sense to call on someone who's been through the process a few times before and knows how to avoid the pitfalls.

Hiring a designer doesn't mean that you hand over the whole process to someone else. A designer is someone who should work *with you* to design your kitchen (or bathroom, or basement, or whatever you're working on). A designer needs your input because you're the expert on how you live your life, and therefore on what you need in terms of design. They should ask about your lifestyle (for instance, how much cooking do you actually do?), who does the cooking, your cooking habits (lots of baking as well as cooking?), your personal sense of style (modern, traditional, eclectic, etc.), your budget, and your long-term goals for the house (starter home, dream home, etc.).

An experienced designer should know the principles of kitchen design like the back of their hand, and should apply them when coming up with layout options for you. Keep in mind, though, that many designers seem to feel most comfortable working in a fairly narrow range of styles, and you'll want to know if their style matches yours before you begin. By looking at their design portfolio, you'll get a sense of whether you share their tastes. You should bring your ideas to the table too, and together you can create a layout and selection of colours and materials that will give you the effect you're looking for. It should be a collaboration.

Who do you choose?

There are a lot of people out there calling themselves designers or decorators.

The words "interior designer" mean that the person has a university degree in interior design, and several years of on-the-job experience. In most parts of Canada, you have to meet the requirements of your provincial association of interior designers to use the title.

A "certified kitchen designer" also has a combination of education and experience, though there's a lot more emphasis on experience than classroom education. The certification part comes from the National Kitchen & Bath Association. Some kitchen design consultants at big box stores will be certified by this association.

The words "designer," "decorator," or "interior decorator" can be used by anyone with any level of training or education. These titles don't tell you much about the person's credentials. It's possible that you'll find someone really talented and experienced who uses one of these titles, but be careful, and make sure you check out lots of references. It's the same process as hiring a contractor.

When interviewing design professionals, make sure you ask these questions:

- **How long have you been in the business?**
- **What are your credentials?**
- **How long does the process take and what's included in your fee?**
- **How and when do you expect to be paid?**
- **Do you work in a particular style, and if so, please describe it.**
- **Can you show me samples of your work?**
- **Can you give me the names and contact information of at least five previous clients?**
- **Can you give me references from contractors you've worked with?**

Many types of work and pay structures are possible. Because I think the contractor is the second-most important person (after you, the homeowner) in a renovation, I think you should find the best possible contractor first, then work with a designer that your contractor recommends. You can go in the other direction, though—that is, find a great designer, and then match the designer up with a contractor.

Here's the challenge when working with designers: the designer needs to understand and respect the contractor's role. The contractor has to build whatever plans the designer comes up with. The contractor will probably be the one who has to arrange for building code inspections, and getting everything passed (although it's ultimately the homeowner's responsibility). If the designer sells you a project design that can't be built, the contractor loses. That explains why the contractor's input during the planning and design stage is absolutely vital—and it also explains why

If you bring in a designer to help plan your kitchen, be sure that your designer works closely with your contractor. Elaborate kitchens, like this one with two islands and a vaulted ceiling, have their own challenges.

designers, architects, engineers, and contractors don't always get along. Be prepared for lots of consultation and different opinions if these various types of professionals are going to be involved in your project.

As for payment, you could pay a one-time fee for the designer to draw up several layouts for consideration, or pay a percentage of the overall cost of the project if the designer remains on the job throughout the construction process. Any of these arrangements could work, as long as you spell it out clearly from the start—as you would with any other member of your renovation team.

If you want to save on design fees, but still get some design input, consider a hybrid approach. Many of the big box stores offer free in-store consultation. They can be a big help in planning the layout and even choosing finishes (such as countertops, backsplashes, and faucets), but don't expect to find the most innovative design advice if you decide to go this route. You also have to remember that any designer working for a big box store will be creating designs that use only products and brands carried by that store. That may be a problem if you're looking for something truly unique, but you're always free to use other products or brands that you have in mind.

MIKE'S TIP

Basics for every kitchen
Layout basics

Think of the kitchen in terms of distinct areas for different functions: food storage, food preparation, cooking, and dish washing.

1. **Wherever possible, use the work triangle as your guide for positioning the three major workstations (refrigerator, stovetop or range, and sink). Measured from the centre of each of these stations, each side of the triangle should be at least 4 feet in length, and no more than 9 feet. For the most efficient layout, the total perimeter of the triangle should be at least 12 feet and no more than 26 feet. The purpose of this rule is to minimize the number of steps needed from point to point.**
2. **Where there's an aisle between two runs of cabinets (or an island), allow a minimum of 42 inches. Allow at least 48 inches if the kitchen is for two or more people to work in.**
3. **Ensure that all appliances and doors can open fully, without blocking throughways or bumping into cupboards or other appliances.**
4. **In a U-shaped kitchen, don't locate two workstations directly opposite one another. This avoids having two people working back to back to each other.**

Refrigerator

Locate the refrigerator as close to the main kitchen entrance as possible. It's easier for bringing groceries in, and it also allows others to access the refrigerator while leaving the main work area (and the cook) undisturbed.

Leave counter space on at least one side of the refrigerator for unloading groceries and for placing things when you're removing them from the refrigerator.

Stovetop, oven, and range hood

Leave at least 24 inches of counter space on at least one side (and preferably both sides) of the cooking surface. This allows room for food prep and ingredients, and a place to set hot pots and pans as you cook or remove items from the oven.

In front of the oven, leave a clear floor space that measures at least 30 inches by 48 inches. Wall ovens, set at eye level, minimize back strain for the cook, and are safer for children than range ovens that are closer to floor level.

The distance between your range hood and your stove top depends on the type of element. For a gas stove, the height should be 30 inches minimum, or higher if you have a grill too.

Centre a ventilator hood (fan) over the stovetop and position it a minimum of 25 inches and a maximum of 30 inches above it. For gas stoves, set the hood at the higher measurement.

The ventilator hood should have a cubic-feet-per-minute (CFM) rating of at least 150. It should be higher if your stovetop includes a grill or griddle unit.

Sink and dishwasher

Leave counter space of at least 24 inches on both sides of the sink. Double-basin sinks give you more flexibility than single, but a second sink for prep work (placed in the island, for example) can give you the same benefit.

Place the dishwasher next to the sink for easier cleanup, with a clear work surface above it for stacking and unloading dishes.

The height of a kitchen island depends on whether you're using it for preparation or eating.

Position the sink at least 24 inches from the cooking surface. You can easily reach running water while cooking, and can fill or empty pots and pans as needed.

Place the sink under a window. The vast majority of people prefer to wash dishes with a view in front of them, and the natural light is useful for cleanup. Ensure that the faucet, when in use, will not get in the way of opening the window.

Kitchen dining: Table or island

If you plan to have an eat-in kitchen, allow at least 48 inches from each edge of the table to any cabinets or appliances. This keeps the dining space from being cramped.

At an island or bar-height counter, allow room for knees to fit comfortably underneath. For a bar height of 44 inches, choose stools that measure about 30 inches. For a bar height of 36 inches, choose stools about 24 inches high.

MIKE'S TIP

Plan ahead with universal design

Planning a kitchen or bathroom renovation means more than just choosing paint co-lours and cabinetry or deciding whether stainless-steel appliances are out of style. You need to look beyond the surfaces and focus on the long term. One way to do this is by incorporating the principles of universal design into your plan.

You may have heard the phrase "universal design" and thought it meant making spaces more accessible to people with disabilities. Or perhaps you've read about it in connection with "aging in place"—being able to live comfort-ably, safely, and independently in your home for many years to come. These are aspects of universal design, but it's about a lot more.

Simply put, the point of universal design is to create a home that works for everyone at all stages of life—regardless of age, height, or physical capability. At its best, it provides benefits you may not immediately think of. For example, wider doorways are obviously good for people in wheelchairs, but they're also helpful if you're pushing a baby stroller or want to move a bulky piece of furniture into the house. Someone with arthritis in their hands will find a levered door han-dle easier to use than a round doorknob, but so will children, who have smaller hands. Stovetops with controls on the front are easier for everyone to reach; they're also safer, because you don't have to reach past a hot pot or burner to adjust the temperature. Anti-slip flooring made of cork has the added benefit of being naturally resistant to moisture and mould.

You may worry that you'll end up with a kitchen or bathroom that looks insti-tutional, but manufacturers are taking the "design" part of the equation to heart, developing products that are both functional and attractive. And universal design doesn't have to be expensive. Choices such as C- or D-shaped handles for cabinets or a handheld shower head are pretty low-cost ways of gaining some of the benefits of universal design. In an older house, there's a pretty good chance you'll have to gut the kitchen or bathroom you're remodelling, which presents an opportunity to install features such as multi-level countertops, walk- or roll-in showers, or cabinets with pull-out shelves.

As you plan to introduce universal design concepts into your kitchen or bath-room renovation, think about who lives in the house—their ages, their heights, and any physical limitations they face. But don't stop there; think also about any friends or family members who visit frequently—what are their needs? And con-sider how long you plan to live in your home. The longer that time frame is, the more it makes sense to add elements that will help you "age in place."

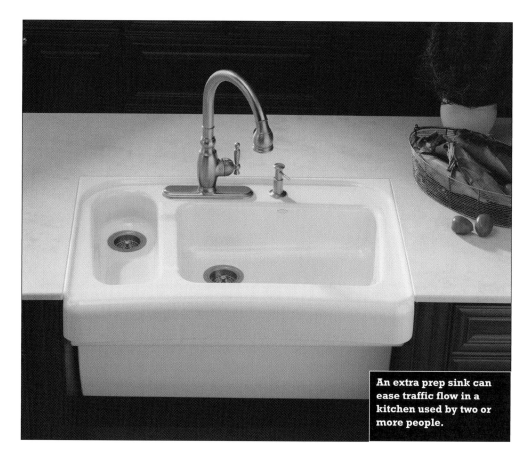

An extra prep sink can ease traffic flow in a kitchen used by two or more people.

The nuts and bolts of outfitting your kitchen

Not so long ago, if you wanted to buy specialty foods you had to go to a specialty food store. These days, most grocery stores carry all kinds of foods. What used to be available to only a few people, and usually only in big cities, is now available to almost everyone, everywhere.

The same has happened with everything that goes into building a kitchen. From cabinetry to appliances, it's easier than ever to find a source for those high-end products you see in the "shelter" magazines. Want a professional-style, six-burner gas range? A built-in espresso machine? Thousands of cabinet styles and finishes to choose from? These days, it's a case of "you want it, you got it."

The result of all this good stuff is that consumers have lots of choices. Sometimes too many. When you're facing a major overhaul of your kitchen, it's easy to feel overwhelmed by everything that's available in the marketplace, especially when manufacturers are always trying to sell you on the special, "innovative" features their products have.

MIKE'S TIP

Smart choices for appliances

Look for the Energy Star symbol. Manufacturers have made great advances in producing more energy-efficient appliances. They've improved the insulation and thermostats in refrigerators, and designed dishwashers that need less water. In 2004, the average refrigerator or dishwasher used less than half as much power as in 1990.

Don't overwork your fridge, and let it breathe. Placing refrigerators near heat sources such as ovens, forced-air registers, or radiators forces them to work harder. Direct sunlight shining on a fridge through a window has the same effect. And don't forget that the fridge's own compressor and condensing coils are sources of heat, so we need to leave room for this heat to escape.

Think about an induction cooktop. They're more expensive, but they do the job faster, plus they're more energy efficient and safer. The heat goes into the pan, not the kitchen. Beneath the flat-top surface of the range, a coil of copper wire works as an electromagnet when current is passed through it. Energy is transferred to the metal surface of a pot or pan, where it is converted into heat. There's no open flame or heated elements to present a burning hazard. One drawback is that you can only use steel or iron cookware—copper or aluminum pots aren't magnetic and therefore won't work well with this technology.

"Professional" isn't the same as "professional-style." You may want the look of a restaurant kitchen, so you might be tempted to buy a real commercial range online, second-hand, or from a restaurant-supply store. Don't. There are big differences between professional ranges and professional-style models designed for use in the home. A true professional range isn't insulated the same way, so you'll need at least three inches of space between it and the surrounding cabinets. The knobs on a commercial range aren't child safe, and the ovens usually don't have windows, lights, or broilers. Some insurance companies won't cover you if you have a commercial range in your home, and some municipalities won't allow them. You can still have the look of a restaurant kitchen; just be sure to get appliances actually built for home use.

Cabinets

Cabinets are the most important, and most expensive, part of your kitchen renovation. This is where the quality, or lack of it, is most easily hidden. On the surface, most kitchen cabinets look fabulous. Underneath, I have seen some of the worst crap imaginable being sold for criminal prices. You need to see beyond the fancy doors and pretty knobs so you can be sure you're getting cabinets that are made right.

The carcass

The biggest drop in quality over the years in cabinet making has been with the boxes behind the doors (the carcass). In the 1960s, most kitchen cabinet carcasses were made

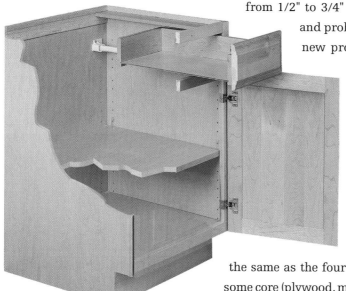

from 1/2" to 3/4" plywood—incredibly strong and durable and probably overbuilt. As material costs rose and new products like particleboard, melamine, and medium-density fibreboard came along and lower grades of plywood were produced, the carcass became the obvious place for manufacturers to save money.

The carcass is usually made of two materials—one for the four sides (the left and right, the top, and the bottom)—and another, thinner material, for the back. The shelves can end up being made of a third material, but most often they're the same as the four sides. Typically, the carcass is made from some core (plywood, melamine, particleboard, or medium-density fibreboard) covered with a thin veneer of wood.

Every kitchen cabinet starts as a carcass (the box), so the material used and the way it's built are what separates the cheap cabinets from the top-quality ones.

You've got to know what you're paying for. Plywood with a veneer (veneer core) is still the best material, but it's expensive—even the mid-range veneer cores cost up to three times as much as melamine. That means a kitchen cabinet set that would cost $15,000 in melamine would cost about $26,000 in mid-range veneer.

Of the kitchens available today, 90% are melamine veneer—chances are that's what you're going to be looking at.

What matters with a melamine carcass is how it's constructed. Butt-jointed, glued, and stapled melamine carcasses are the lowest of the low. The glue doesn't stick to melamine and staples rely on the glue to hold the carcass together. A carcass like that will fall apart. Anyone that builds them shouldn't be in business.

The carcass should be at least 5/8" thick. The joints should be rabbeted so the glue has contact with raw particleboard on both pieces and provides structural strength.

MIKE'S TIP

And forget the staples. Particleboard doesn't hold screws very well, let alone staples. The best way to connect the sides is with wooden or steel dowels. Wooden dowels, when glued, provide tons of mechanical connection. Steel dowels rely on themselves to make a strong connection. You want dowelled carcass sides if you've got a melamine carcass.

The carcass backs are often made from 1/8" Masonite, but I would only accept half an inch at a minimum. More importantly, the Masonite should be let into the back, not surface mounted. The back plays a big part in stabilizing the whole cabinet. Staples and glue are okay here, but there have to be plenty of staples. It has to be very firm. There should be no flex at all.

The drawers

Where there are drawers, there should be additional stretchers (horizontal pieces of solid wood that stabilize the two sides of the cabinet) in the carcass between the drawers. Sometimes there are none, or they're just at the top and bottom.

Hardware matters: the quality of the drawer slides varies a lot, and here, you get what you pay for. The best slides are designed to be installed under the drawer and they're more expensive than side sliders, which are cheaper and less durable. There are some slider systems that use plastic drawers where the only part that's wood is the drawer face. I think they're just ugly.

The best wood drawers are 3/4" plywood or solid wood, with the backs let into the sides, not butt jointed. The drawer bottoms should be 1/4" plywood and slide into grooves along

Dovetail joints are the strongest joints for drawers, but they also require the highest skill level to make.

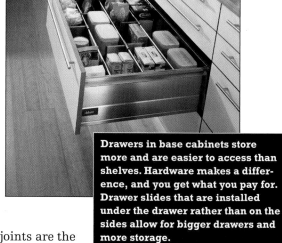

Drawers in base cabinets store more and are easier to access than shelves. Hardware makes a difference, and you get what you pay for. Drawer slides that are installed under the drawer rather than on the sides allow for bigger drawers and more storage.

the sides, not stuck on the bottom. Dovetail joints are the best choice. Anytime dowels, biscuits, or finger joint corners are used to connect drawer components, you're looking at a well-made drawer, so be sure to ask how your drawers are built.

Doors

Cabinet doors come in all kinds of materials. The trouble is, on the showroom floor they all look pretty much the same quality. Why? Because if they're painted or coated in solid colours you can't see the method of construction.

Clear-finished wood doors are usually what we call "five-piece." That means they're a frame of two rails (horizontal pieces) and two stiles (vertical pieces), with a raised panel inset. The rails and stiles should be jointed and fit perfectly in what's called a "cope and stick" joint. Look at the corners where the profiles meet. They should line up perfectly. There's no excuse for gaps or fillers. The panel should be set into the frame, not stuck on the back.

Door finishes

Painted doors with a profile come in a variety of materials. Most are medium-density fibreboard—not my favourite—but it's the finish that really matters. The cheapest is thermofused. That's a medium-density fibreboard door that has a PVC film heated and vacuumed to the face of the door. Next is oil-based paint. Both are cheap and the finishes don't last. The best reasonably priced finish is a high-quality, catalyzed lacquer. The top of the line is a polyvinyl finish. It looks great and lasts forever.

Cabinet hardware

Hardware varies quite a bit also, but the standard for hinges has become the Blum hinge. They're great hinges, but now you have to look at how the cabinets are installed.

Cabinet upgrades that are worth the splurge

Quiet-close or soft-close drawers and cabinet doors

Impossible to slam, these drawers and cabinets close almost automatically and help keep the noise level down in your kitchen and stop fingers from getting pinched.

Quality hardware

Look for high-quality knobs, hinges, handles, and pulls in unique and attractive materials such as brushed nickel, solid nickel, stainless steel, bronze, or wood, rather than plastic. These all add to your kitchen and if it's good quality, it will last.

The hinges allow for enough flexibility that no door should look crooked or out of line with the rest of the doors. If they do, it's a symptom of a bad installation.

Installation

Even the best-quality cabinets can look like garbage if they aren't properly installed. During and after installation, look at how the cabinets are connected to the wall. They have to be level. Your doors and drawers should open easily without touching anything else. Make sure filler strips are used in between cabinets—that's essential. If it doesn't look right, more than likely it isn't, and you should talk to your general contractor about it. This is important. I've seen cabinets hung so poorly that it's a miracle they didn't pull out of the wall and fall on the homeowner.

Lighting the kitchen

Today's kitchens aren't just for cooking and eating, they're also a place to entertain and relax, and often they have a desk for paying bills and for the kids to do homework. It makes sense that you're going to need more than one kind of lighting. How and where you use lighting can really make or break your kitchen.

The most obvious—and least expensive—source of light is natural light coming from

What can happen when cabinets are installed wrong and not even screwed into studs.

windows and skylights, so of course you want to maximize the natural light in your kitchen. (See more on windows and skylights starting on page 51.)

There are different types of lighting, usually divided into three basic categories: general or ambient lighting (such as overhead lights, chandeliers, or other dining table lights), task lighting (brighter lights used over the sink, island, or other work stations), and accent lighting (such as pot lights around the perimeter of the room, track lighting, or wall sconces). A single type of fixture—such as track lights, for instance—can fit into more than one category, depending on how it's used.

General or ambient lighting

General lighting in the kitchen is likely to take the form of a single overhead ceiling fixture. This could be track lighting, or any number of ceiling fixtures, usually with multiple bulbs. With LED (light-emitting-diodes), which casts a very direct and focussed light, you'll need a fixture that has a number of bulbs to get the wash of light that you're looking for, and enough illumination for the whole room.

Keep the proportions of the room in mind as you choose an overhead fixture: too large or too small will look strange. Too much light will make the room so bright that

A common thing that people forget in a kitchen is lighting. Think about task lighting such as under-cabinet lighting, direct overhead lighting that doesn't shadow you as you work at a counter, and lighting over an island.

LED lighting

Mention energy-efficient lighting and most people think of compact fluorescent lamps, or CFLs. But CFLs contain mercury, they take time to reach full brightness, their flickering can be annoying, and the quality of light they give isn't to everyone's taste. There's another option: light-emitting diodes, or LEDs. You've seen them for years in the digital display on your alarm clock, the tail lights of your car, and in strings of Christmas tree lights. And they're being used more and more around the house.

LEDs are even more energy efficient than CFLs, and they last longer too—roughly 10 times as long as CFLs, and between 50 and 100 times as long as incandescent bulbs. Unlike incandescents, which use electric current to heat a filament until it glows and gives off light and lots of heat, LEDs pass electricity through a semiconductor material. More than 80% of the energy is turned into light, while generating next to no heat.

Because LED light is highly directional—that is, it shines where it's pointed instead of spreading in all directions—it has traditionally been used for task lighting. In kitchens, LED fixtures are excellent over work spaces like the stove, sink, or island. They're also a very good choice for accent lighting, installed under the cabinets, or for mood lighting. Some new products are ideal for cove lighting too, and are even dimmable.

But just like CFLs, LEDs have their downside. You may find the light too cold or too intense—LEDs don't provide that yellowish glow you get from incandescents. And they are certainly more expensive, although prices are coming down, and you come out ahead on the electricity you save; LEDs pay for themselves in a couple of years.

I've used LEDs on many projects, including my own home. They're worth looking into as you plan your renovation.

you'll never want to turn the overhead light on, but if you don't have enough light you'll be disappointed.

Task lighting

In a kitchen, task lighting may be the most important kind. You need strong, clear light for preparing food, cooking, washing dishes, dining, and so on. But because task lighting tends to be stronger than any other kind, it can create what are called "hot spots" (areas that are too bright), and the opposite, which are known as "dead areas." Ambient lighting and accent lighting help to fill in the gaps and even out the light in the room.

Over an island or other work area, consider pendant fixtures for direct, even light. The most common error when buying a pendant light is to go too small. You can also use several pendants together if you don't want to go with a really large fixture.

A few other things to think about when you're choosing light fixtures: In a dining room or any eating area, the size of the table matters. The diameter of the fixture overhead should be about one-third the length of your table. And in a dining room, it's best to "go low": most of us hang our fixtures too close to the ceiling. The idea is to hang the fixture just over the heads of your guests. That works for an island in the kitchen as well. Choose a fixture for the dining table that doesn't have light bulbs exposed from below, or you'll all be looking into a bare light bulb while you eat.

If there's a desk or office area in your kitchen, you'll need a dedicated light, and maybe a task light for the computer. Recessed downlights can work as task lights as long as they're large enough and positioned directly over the work area.

Accent lighting

Accent lighting gives focused light that highlights important areas in the room. You can do this with a series of recessed lights, or with wall sconces or other fixtures that give focused light. For a while now, recessed lights have been the most popular type of accent lighting, and that's a good thing. They're versatile (you can use them for almost any kind of space), and the best news is that they are now available with LED technology.

The flexibility of recessed lighting

Recessed lighting sizes range from 3 to 8 inches in diameter. These are usually referred to as "can"-type fixtures. You'll see that they're made of a metal housing (that's the can part) with a plastic or metal trim that gives it a finished look. Trims are available in lots of different styles and colours, so you can make the lights stand out more (with a trim that contrasts with the ceiling) or almost seem to disappear (with a trim that matches the ceiling). Here are some ways to use recessed lights:

- **Recessed lights in the ceiling, around the perimeter of the kitchen, will give the whole room an even glow.**
- **One or more recessed ceiling lights can be positioned to draw attention to artwork, dishes, or cookbooks on shelves.**
- **Glass-fronted cabinets for displaying dishes will stand out more with built-in recessed lights.**
- **Recessed under-cabinet lights make the counter space more practical.**
- **Over-cabinet lights accent ceilings and add drama, especially where walls and ceiling meet at unusual angles.**

MIKE'S TIP

Insulation makes a difference with recessed lighting.

Before you have recessed lights installed, make sure you and your contractor know what's in the space above where the lights will go. Is it a heated, fully indoor space, such as an insulation-free joist cavity between two levels in a house? This is likely the case with a main-floor kitchen or bathroom (unless you have soundproofing insulation between levels). If there's no insulation in a heated area, any kind of recessed fixture will do just fine, as long as it's installed properly, with nothing touching the fixture.

But if your recessed fixtures are going to be surrounded by insulation—in a cold attic, for instance—then you absolutely must use a fixture that bears the IC designation. These letters stand for the words "in contact." This means the fixtures are safe even when they're completely shrouded in insulation. In addition to being rated for safe insulation contact, IC fixtures are designed to prevent warm, moist indoor air from leaking up through the light and condensing in the attic space during winter. IC fixtures are sealed; if it weren't for this key feature, frost and water would develop above them during cold weather, damaging the light and your home. Make sure your contractor uses the right fixture for the job.

Once you've identified the effect you want to achieve, you need to determine what size and type of fixture will get you to your goal. If your room needs a wide beam of light for general lighting, then consider a fixture that uses a 120-volt, flood-style light bulb. This is the so-called high-voltage option and is also the simplest. The hardware is inexpensive, dimmer switches are cheap, and replacement bulbs have the usual screw-type Edison base of the sort found on light bulbs everywhere.

High-voltage recessed fixtures are often large and they look really obvious. That's why designers created smaller, low-voltage light systems. The most popular of these use an MR16 bulb. With a face diameter of just 2 inches, these small, 12-volt bulbs give off more light than you might think.

Low-voltage fixtures need a transformer to step down 120-volt household current, but what you get in return is greater visual options, especially in the MR16 category. These fixtures usually come with bulb options and choices for light beams and radius.

The "rules" for placing recessed light fixtures

The basic sizes for recessed lights are 4, 5, or 6 inches in diameter. The 6" fixtures can be used in tall entryways or two-storey hallways, while the smaller 4" ones work better in smaller spaces since they don't stand out as much. Match the size of your recessed lighting fixtures to how close together they can be installed. The common rule is that 4" fixtures should be placed at least 4 feet apart and 6" fixtures about 6 feet apart.

Centre recessed lighting fixtures in front of the objects you want to light—a painting, a bookshelf, or drapes, for example—and about 12 to 18 inches in front of that object, when you measure along the ceiling.

Recessed lights used for reading or task lighting should be carefully placed overhead so your head and shoulders will not block needed light.

For under-cabinet lighting, plan to install a continuous row of lights for the most evenly distributed light. Under-cabinet lighting is available in several varieties: LED, fluorescent or halogen strips, and individual "puck"-style halogen fixtures. Fluorescent fixtures are less expensive than halogen, but halogen provides a light that's a bit more like sunlight. LED fixtures that cast a more natural light are now also available.

Some under-cabinet areas may not need an entire strip of lights. In such cases, small, individual puck-shaped LED lights are ideal.

Lighting controls for flexibility

Once you have installed multiple lights of different types, you need to control them, both separately and in groups, to get the most flexibility.

Lighting controls should be placed at any entrance to the kitchen, as well as at key work areas such as desk alcoves, islands, etc. Some people like the infrared remote control units that allow you to control your lighting much the same way as you control your television.

Timers and electronic sensors—with motion detectors, for instance—that turn lights on and off automatically are also becoming more popular in the kitchen. Dimmer switches, even though they've been around for a long time, are still a cheap and effective way to control how much light a fixture puts out.

Other electrical needs in the kitchen

A good design in your kitchen involves planning for lighting, as we've just discussed, but your kitchen has other electrical needs too, such as outlets (how many and where), ventilation, and even in-floor heat. Your general contractor and electrical contractor need to know exactly what you want in order to deliver it to you. Ask yourself the following questions, and make sure your final drawing and written plan for the kitchen answer all of them.

Where do the outlets need to be located for your new kitchen layout? Consider the height of cabinetry and appliances, especially if you're thinking of going with base cabinets that are higher than standard, since this will affect the placement of outlets.

What appliances do you want to accommodate? Think about a microwave, wine fridge, kettle, indoor grill (if separate from your cooktop), blender, mixer, waffle maker, etc. Have a plan for where each one of these will be used, and where the outlets will go. Your fridge needs to be on a separate electrical circuit.

What kind of wiring will you need, now and in the future, for a telephone, a television, stereo speakers, or computer equipment in the kitchen? Have wiring installed where you know you need it right now. I also recommend running some 1½" ABS piping right through the house during your renovation so that you'll be able to fish any type of wiring through it in the future.

What are your plans for lighting? I've just walked you through a discussion on the different types of lighting (general or ambient lighting, task lighting, and accent lighting). Now's the time to finalize your decisions about how much light you want, and where it should be placed. Plan for flexibility.

Will your range be powered by electricity or gas? The electrical outlet and circuit required for an electric stove is much larger than an everyday outlet (50 amps rather than 20 amps), so planning ahead is essential.

What type of range hood will you have installed? Ventilation is essential in kitchens for removing moisture and odours. The size of the range or cooktop will determine how large a range hood you need. I recommend venting a range hood directly to the outside, with as few bends and turns in the vent pipe as possible. (See more on kitchen fans in the sidebar on page 116.)

Are you planning to use ceiling fans? Be aware that special wiring and framing in the ceiling will be needed. Ceiling fans are often sold in combination with a light fixture. Do you want the fan and light to operate on separate switches? Make sure your electrician knows what you want.

Do you want any devices (lights or receptacles) on three-way switches? This allows you to flip the switch from more than one location, which is particularly useful at different entrances to the same room, or at the top and bottom of stairs. It's a safety and convenience feature that's not easy to add once the reno is done.

Will your kitchen have an island? If so, plan for at least one, and preferably more, electrical outlets to be installed within the island. Wiring can be run through the cabinetry or the legs.

Are you planning to use electrical in-floor radiant heat in your kitchen? If so, your electrician needs to know this ahead of time so they can provide the necessary wiring. It has to be wired directly to the electrical panel on a dedicated circuit.

Your final drawing—whether done by you or by a licensed designer or architect—should show the location (including distance from the floor) of every outlet and light fixture. Your electrician will be able to determine which outlets need to be GFCIs (ground fault circuit interrupters), which are a necessary safety feature within 3 feet of a water source, so this is important for both kitchens and bathrooms.

MIKE'S TIP

Before that new range hood goes in...

There are many different types of range hoods, and some of them are pretty impressive to look at. But a range hood—really, it's a large fan—should do more than make a design statement. Its real purpose is to exhaust moist air and cooking odours to the outside. There are pros and cons to each style of fan, whether you go with the most common under-cabinet type, or with the pricier wall-mounted fans. Over-the-range microwave/fan combinations are great space-savers, but the fan may not have the quality you really need. For cooktops located in an island, you can choose from ceiling-mounted fans or downdraft fans. Downdraft fans keep the space looking clean, since there's no apparatus above the cooktop, but think about it: hot air rises, so how efficient can a fan be if it's pulling air from the same level as the stove itself? Some downdraft fans are built into a unit that pops up behind or to the side of the cooking surface, and can be moved back down when they're not in use, and those designs may be more efficient.

With any fan, look for a CFM (cubic feet per minute) rating, which measures the volume of exhaust, of at least 150, and choose a fan that's quiet when it's operating. Noise is measured in sones; one sone is roughly the same as a running refrigerator, and even a small increase can mean the fan is much louder. Two sones is twice as loud as one sone. Why does it matter? If your fan is too loud, you're less likely to use it. To get good exhaust and low noise, you will have to spend some money. You don't want to buy the cheapest model of fan.

Before you buy a fan, talk to your contractor about what will work best in terms of venting. Exhaust lines for your fan may also need to be adjusted, whether you've got an electric stove or a gas stove going into your new kitchen. In the past, exhaust lines were only 4 inches in diameter, whereas most new range hoods require a 6″ line. Exhaust lines work best when they're short, straight runs. The longer they are and the more corners there are, the less efficient the fan will be. Having a 90-degree turn in the exhaust line is like adding an extra 10 feet of run. For the same reason, flexible lines should be avoided.

You should also talk to your HVAC specialist. Installing a huge fan could create a lot of negative air pressure in the house if there isn't fresh air coming in.

Whatever you do, avoid recirculating fans. What's the point of moving dirty air around? Always vent directly to the outside.

The kitchen sink

Things to consider when choosing a kitchen sink include material, shape, and colour, as well as how the sink will be mounted. Choose your sink shape based on the way you use your kitchen and the things you do most often. How the sink is mounted (drop-in or some version of undermount) is a matter of taste, and also of what works best with your countertop material. The most common sink materials available today are stainless steel, porcelain, acrylic, and solid-surface.

Installing an undermount sink requires more precision than a top-mounted one because the cutout has to be exact. Your contractor should install brackets under your sink to help support the weight.

Stainless steel sinks are the most popular, and for good reason: they can be fairly low cost, durable, and relatively lightweight. If you tend to be hard on your sink—prone to throwing things into it—stainless is the best choice. Stainless steel sinks are available in several different sizes and thicknesses, which means their weight will vary.

Stainless steel is graded by gauge; the lower the gauge number, the thicker and heavier the sink. A stainless steel sink with a gauge higher than 18 should be avoided, because a higher number means thinner steel. The thinner the steel, the more likely it is to dent or scratch easily. Stainless steel sinks can be noisy when you're putting dishes or pots into them, so look for a sink that has an undercoating to muffle sound.

You can easily find a durable and attractive stainless steel sink without seams or rims, made from one solid sheet of steel. Possibly the number one advantage of a stainless steel sink is how easy it is to keep clean. This is especially true for a seamless sink, which has no cracks or crevices for bacteria and other grime to hide in. With no special care required other than regular cleaning, a stainless steel sink will keep its appearance for a long time.

A top-mounted stainless steel corner sink. Stainless steel is measured in gauges and it can be confusing. The lower the gauge, the thicker the steel. A 16-gauge steel sink is thicker than an 18-gauge one.

In addition to steel, it's possible to get sinks made of various metals. Nickel, copper, and brass are all available for the kitchen, as well as specialty sinks. Used for generations, these other types of metal sinks can be great looking, but also expensive. Nickel is harder and stronger than copper. Copper is particularly popular at the moment. Over time, it ages and gets a dark patina like an old penny. It requires virtually no maintenance. Used for centuries in Europe, copper sinks have been shown to kill *E. coli* bacteria in a matter of hours, while the same bacteria can linger for days in a stainless steel sink. A copper sink should be pure copper and it should be welded, not soldered. A soldered sink will turn black at the joints and look ugly as it ages.

Porcelain enamel over cast iron is one of the most durable options for kitchen sinks and has been used for more than a hundred years. It has a wide range in quality, style, and colour, and is available for undermount, self-rimming, and tile-in installations. A high-quality sink of this type could last you twenty-five to thirty years or more. The surface is ground glass melted and applied to the hot cast iron. If you drop a heavy pot the wrong way, the porcelain could chip. Porcelain sinks can be resurfaced, though, for less than it costs to replace them.

Beyond the traditional stainless steel and porcelain, kitchen sinks are also manufactured from engineered materials, which include everything from a solid-surface product like Corian to quartz-, slate-, or granite-acrylic composites as well as cast acrylic.

Solid-surface materials can be integrated into the countertop (even if the sink and countertop are different colours), which is the ultimate in easy cleaning and moisture control. If you opt for a solid-surface sink that's separate from the counter, you'll have a wide variety of colours to choose from. Solid-surface materials can also mimic granite and other high-end stones. There are no grooves or seams, so there's no place for kitchen waste crud to collect.

Composite stone sinks are starting to gain popularity. They're made of various types of rock, including quartz, granite, or slate, and combined with acrylic. They're very hard but are warm to the touch, have a matte finish, and don't scratch easily.

Installing the sink

Top mounting (sometimes called a drop-in sink) is the easiest method of installation and requires the least expertise. A self-rimming sink is just placed into a hole that's been cut out of the countertop, and the sink is then fastened with hardware under the counter. Your installer should seal the edge with silicone caulking to prevent crud from getting underneath. This is especially important if your countertop is a laminate; the inner core of pressboard will be destroyed in no time if it gets wet.

Undermount sinks are more difficult to install, but are much more practical since you wipe your counter right into your sink. Undermount sinks used to require a solid-surface countertop or stone, but today there are undermount sinks that can be installed in a laminate countertop.

Flush-mount sinks sit even with the countertop. There's no lip as with a self-rimming sink, so the look is cleaner. You can get the same look with an integrated sink—a countertop and sink unit all in one piece.

Farmhouse sinks (also called apron sinks) feature an exposed front that sometimes juts past the front of the cabinetry that surrounds it. They're commonly used in kitchens with a rustic or country-style feel, and the sinks are usually deeper than average. They often have no deck (the flat part behind the bowl), so the faucet and other accessories are mounted directly into the countertop behind the bowl.

This sink combines the traditional apron front with up-to-the-minute brushed stainless steel.

When you buy a new sink, you have to determine how many holes you'll need in the deck. Depending on the style of faucet you choose, you'll need one to three holes to accommodate the taps and spigot. You can either buy the sink with the correct number of holes, or have the necessary number drilled before it leaves the store. More holes will be needed if you want options like a hot water dispenser, a spray accessory (if it's not integrated into the faucet), or a built-in soap dispenser. It's difficult to add holes once the sink is in place, so get as many as you think you'll ever need. Special accessories are available to camouflage holes that aren't being used. A sink with the drain hole placed farther back than the usual centre position frees up space underneath by pushing the water lines farther to the back of the cabinet.

The kitchen faucet

The faucet is something you're going to use a lot, so it makes sense to budget accordingly and choose a high-quality faucet. This is another place in the kitchen where you can easily make a difference to the environment, and new faucet technology can help.

Faucets can be wall-mounted or installed on your counter. Don't install faucets on an outside wall.

Like every other part of a kitchen today, faucets have evolved. They're available in more shapes, styles, and finishes, and with more functions than ever. Get to know what's on the market before you make your choice.

Pot-fillers faucets, like the ones in restaurants, can be plumbed into your home kitchen.

First let's look at what makes a good faucet. You should know that you have to pay a certain amount to get the best-quality brands, but after that, you're just paying for looks or a more expensive exterior metal such as nickel, brass, or gold. The internal workings have nothing to do with the kind of metal you see on the outside of the faucet.

Every faucet has a mechanism for controlling water flow. The best faucets contain a cartridge housing a pair of ceramic disks. Each disk has holes in it. Turning the faucet's handle slides the disks over one another, lining up the holes so the water can flow through the cartridge and out the faucet. Turning the faucet off moves the holes out of alignment, stopping the flow.

Ceramic disks are extremely hard; if there's any grit or debris in the water, the disks grind it up and remain undamaged. The disks are fired at very high temperatures so even the hottest water can't damage them. The disk faces are highly polished so they stick together as if magnetized. The higher the polish, the smoother they glide and the smoother the faucet handle operates, which gives you control over volume and temperature with less effort. There are other valves on the market—such as the standard ball valve, or the somewhat pricier cartridge valve—but ceramic-disk technology is state of the art.

Another important thing to look for is what the faucet is made of on the inside. The best ones are either solid brass or stainless steel. Both of these metals stand up to high pressure, high temperatures, and potentially corrosive minerals in the water supply. Look for cast—not tubular—brass. Because it will tarnish, brass usually is plated with chrome. Stainless steel doesn't need an additional finish. It's a lot harder to work with, so it will be more expensive than a brass faucet.

The vast majority of faucets sold today have a single control for temperature and volume control. You can save energy by getting one with an aerator, which injects air bubbles into the water stream to achieve the same pressure with less volume, and recirculation pumps to keep hot water at the tap, saving hundreds of gallons a year by eliminating the need to run the tap while the water gets hot.

A convenient feature available on many single-control faucets is the integral spray head, which pulls out from the end of the faucet. The hose for these faucet spray heads requires sturdy construction because the hose often gets some pretty rough treatment in everyday use. The best hoses are either nylon or plastic, protected by an outer covering of woven stainless steel. The woven steel provides stability with its weight and is less likely to kink than unsheathed plastic. The spray heads themselves are usually made of plastic and are finished to match the rest of the faucet.

MIKE'S TIP

Installing sinks and taps the right way

Even the best sink or faucet can end up causing problems if it's not installed the right way. Everything must be absolutely watertight once that sink and faucet are installed.

If your plumber doesn't seal around the faucet and sink with a quality silicone caulking, you could end up with water damage, mould, and rot over time. In fact, a lot of people start thinking about a kitchen renovation because they've noticed that their countertop has completely rotted out from water seeping into it near the sink.

Unfortunately, a lot of plumbers don't take the final step of sealing everything up, and you'll probably have to ask for it. Here's what to ask for.

Around a drop-in sink, where the sink meets the countertop, there should be a thin bead of clear silicone caulking to keep water from getting underneath the lip of the sink. If the water gets under there—and it will get in there, just from everyday use in a kitchen—you're going to have mould. This is especially true if you've got a laminate countertop with a pressed-wood core: that "wood" is just wood fibres held together with glue, and if it gets wet, it gets mouldy in no time. No matter what your cabinets and countertop are made of, you don't want them getting wet all the time, because that water will destroy them.

For faucets, there are three stages to seal them properly. First, the holes that the faucets will drop into should be sealed with a bead of caulking. Then, once the faucet is in place, the holes should be sealed again. Finally, once the escutcheon plates (the finishing plates) go on, a bead of clear caulking should go around the edge. This way, you make sure that water isn't going to drip down into the cabinet. Make sure that your contractor knows you want them to go the extra mile on this to do it right.

Countertops

Countertops are an important part of how your kitchen looks, and there are more choices available than ever. Some high-end materials, like stone, have gotten cheaper, and the lower-end products, like laminates, are looking better than ever, with more realistic-looking patterns that imitate granite. As well, there are more and more eco-friendly options—though, as I've said before, not every product that claims to be green is really eco-friendly.

Function is a good place to start when you're considering a new countertop. Ask yourself how you use your kitchen—a lot, a little, not much at all? Some people want a showstopper in terms of style, but they might not cook all that much. If you do a lot of cooking, you definitely need something that's durable and easy to clean and maintain.

Probably the most important issue with countertops—along with durability and cost—is how porous the different materials are. The countertop is where you're working with raw foods, which means you have to think about keeping the counters as clean as possible. A lot of people don't realize that many types of counters—even the ones that look completely hard and impenetrable, such as granite—are actually really porous. A porous countertop holds germs and bacteria, it gets stained easily, and if you put a hot pot on the surface, it can damage the seal.

Porous materials such as granite and natural stone need to be sealed to make them non-porous, and you'll have to reseal them every year or even every six months in heavily used areas. Choosing different countertops for different areas of the kitchen might be the solution—a nice piece of granite for the breakfast bar countertop, stainless steel around the stovetop or cooktop, butcher block in the prep area, and engineered stone around the sink.

Natural stone (granite, marble, and limestone)

The most popular counter material, natural stone, exists everywhere, and it's different everywhere. Even from the same quarry, no two pieces are alike.

Stainless steel countertops, used in restaurant kitchens, are tough and non-porous, and are probably the most sanitary counter material you can choose. But they can require more maintenance and cleaning than other countertops.

Granite is the most popular stone for counters. It's an extremely hard rock formed by volcanic activity. If you buy the kind called "consistent granite," you'll

Because granite countertops are made from natural stone and cut from a big piece of granite, the colour and pattern can vary widely even on the same piece. If you want a more consistent-looking granite counter-top, you should choose the piece that will be cut into your countertop.

Soapstone countertops are less porous than granite, but softer, so they scratch and chip more easily.

get something with the same pattern throughout. Variegated granite has veins that are different from one piece to another, making it difficult to match sections. It's a good idea to buy stone from a warehouse where you can choose the actual piece of stone you'll be getting. If you order from a sample you just don't know what kinds of irregularities might be in the countertop that's actually delivered to your house. For some people, that's fine, and it's part of the look they want. Granite is very porous and should be treated with a penetrating sealer every six months to prevent stains and keep bacteria from getting into the stone.

Soapstone and slate are a lot softer than granite, but surprisingly enough, they're less porous. Slate is formed from clay on ancient sea beds and generally has a solid grey, black, or green colour. Soapstone, which is made primarily of the mineral talc, has a similar colour but often has light streaks of quartz. Both stones scratch and chip easily, especially on the edges; the marks can be sanded out or left in for character. It's not generally necessary to seal these stones, but applying mineral oil to them now and again will make them look great.

Marble and limestone are less practical for kitchens because they can get stained so easily with food acids, but some homeowners feel that age and use just add to the "patina." Marble is probably the best surface for making pastry, and serious bakers often include a section of marble countertop just for this.

What about the environmental aspect of natural stone? It's a non-renewable resource—meaning that once you've taken it out of the ground, it can never be replaced—and is often shipped from long distances. There are a number of green options that can give you the look of stone without the carbon footprint. Look for products made from concrete and recycled glass that offer an environmentally friendly alternative to natural stone and solid-surface materials. They claim to be non-porous, durable, and heat-resistant, and they're available in standard and custom colours.

Be honest with yourself about maintenance.

Some products require maintenance if they're going to last as long as they should. Natural stone countertops—such as granite or marble—need to be sealed every six months or so. While that may not sound like a lot, you'd be surprised how many people just don't bother to do it, and later they're frustrated because their counter shows stains or other signs of wear.

So be realistic about whether you're likely to do the maintenance that's needed for these premium products. If you're not interested in caring for them year after year, it's better to think about a lower-maintenance material such as a composite stone, solid-surface material, or even a laminate.

Engineered stone

Engineered stone has no fissures, veins, or other imperfections that could compromise the strength of natural stone, or make it hard to match seams. The toughest engineered stone is made from quartz. It won't scratch or stain and is non-porous. Others, the ones derived from marble and other stones, are softer, and some will need to be sealed regularly.

Engineered quartz gives you the look of granite with a consistent colour throughout, is less porous, and needs less maintenance.

Solid surfaces or composites (Corian and other brand names)

This is a great option for a kitchen that gets a lot of use—and for homeowners who don't want the maintenance of regular sealing. Solid-surface counters are made by blending acrylic polymers and stone-derived materials, which are then poured into moulds to create sheets about half an inch thick. These counters are almost impossible to stain, and any scratches can be sanded out—although the sanded area may be more susceptible to staining because it no longer has the factory finish. The colour won't fade, because the pattern runs through the whole material (that's why it's called "solid surface"). Solid surfaces can be moulded into almost any shape, which is why integrated sinks are now possible.

Solid-surface countertops are also a low-maintenance option.

Ceramic and porcelain tiles

Made from pressed clay, ceramic tiles come in a huge variety—smooth glazed, matte finished, hand painted, crackled, and printed. Tiles can be used for countertops but are better suited to the backsplash because the grout is porous and easily stained. Heat isn't a problem for tiles, but they can be easily scratched, and they're hard enough that you'll probably lose a lot of dishes and glasses to breakage.

For some people, the cost savings on tile is enough to convince them that they really want to use it for their countertops. If you're one of these people, make absolutely certain that you use a glazed tile and the whole system under the tile is watertight

(I recommend Schluter's Ditra system over plywood), and make sure there's an epoxy mix in the grout (this is one of the few times I recommend epoxy grout).

Tiles are a green choice to begin with, but for an even greener renovation you could look for tiles that are either recycled from previous sites or made from recycled materials.

Laminates

Laminates cost a fraction of what most other counter options cost, and they get the job done. They're made by binding layers of printed paper and resin under high pressure to create a rigid sheet that can be cut, shaped, and glued onto particleboard or medium-density fibreboard. Because anything can be printed on the paper, you can get the look of natural stone, metal, wood, and even granite. Higher-end laminates like Formica are melamine-based, and the surface colour goes throughout the sheet, making nicks and scratches less likely to be seen; this also eliminates the brown edge where two sheets meet at an angle, especially where the countertop sheet meets the edge strip. On the down side, laminates are susceptible to burns and scratches and the marks are permanent, and the inner core of particleboard is vulnerable to mould and water damage if it ever gets wet. If you make sure that sinks and faucets are well sealed when they're installed (see pages 119 and 124), you can still have a good countertop that will last for many years.

Stainless steel

Stainless steel—an alloy of iron, chromium, and nickel—is the industrial standard for tough, clean counters. In fact, it's probably the most sanitary countertop you can buy. Scratch marks do show, but a random-grain finish will make the scratches less noticeable. A brushed finish is smoother but shows more fingerprints. You should order the best kitchen-grade stainless steel, which is labelled N0.304, also known as government grade.

Copper

Copper is one of the most traditional materials for kitchens, though we don't see a lot of it these days. That "timeless" quality of copper is what makes some people pay a premium price for it—that, and the fact that copper can be a very durable and long-lasting product. You don't want to cheap out on copper, though, because you'll end up with an inferior product that will disappoint you. Look for pure copper, not recycled, if you want a countertop that will look good over the long haul. The thickness of copper is measured by weight, so get something that's at least 48 ounces (equivalent to 16-guage in other metals), and ask for any joints or corners to be copper-welded, not soldered.

In this kitchen the stainless steel sink is seamlessly part of the countertop.

Concrete

Concrete countertops are usually poured on-site and made from a concrete mixture that includes pigments for colour. The top surface is evened out, trowelled smooth, and then left to harden for several days. Concrete countertops may also be made off-site, and then laid on top of the cabinets in sheet form, just like granite or other stone counters. Concrete counters are extremely hard and heat-resistant, but very porous, especially when small cracks appear. If you go this route, you absolutely must seal the concrete properly, and wax the counters every few months or so.

Wood

There are two ways to approach wood counters: One is to treat them like fine furniture, keeping them oiled and sealed and not letting even a butter knife cross the surface. The other is to use them like a butcher block, letting the dents and scratches accumulate over time. For the first option, choose teak (which has resins that repel water naturally), cherry, walnut, or mahogany. Wood has been used as a chopping surface for centuries, partly because it has natural antibacterial properties that make it one of the cleanest and safest surfaces for preparing food. Just install your wood counter away from the sink area. Maple is the traditional choice for a butcher block, but bamboo and mesquite—both fast-growing, renewable sources—are even harder than maple and don't scratch as easily. Some bamboo is even manufactured to look like a solid surface.

Countertops at a glance

Material	Granite, slate, marble	Solid-surface materials (such as Corian)	Plastic laminates (such as Arborite)	Quartz composite	Ceramic or porcelain tile	Concrete	Butcher block	Stainless steel	Paper
Water-resistance	Low—must be sealed frequently	High	High	High	High—but grout's is not; must be sealed	Low—must be sealed frequently	Low	High	Moderate to high
Cost	High	High	Low	Moderate to high	Moderate	High	Moderate to high	High	Moderate to high
Environmental concerns	Uses natural but non-renewable resources	Manufacturing process is not environmentally friendly	Manufacturing process is not environmentally friendly	Manufacturing process is not environmentally friendly, though some natural and recycled materials are used	Uses renewable resources and some recycled materials	Uses natural and renewable resources	Uses natural and renewable resources	Manufacturing process is not environmentally friendly	Uses natural, renewable, and post-consumer recycled materials
Good to know	Once the seal has worn off, these are among the most porous surfaces	Available in almost any colour and profile	Must be well-sealed around faucets and sinks to prevent water damage to particleboard core	One of the most durable and non-porous countertops available	Installation must be absolutely watertight	Fine cracks will appear over time, breaking the seal and trapping bacteria	Wood is porous once seal has worn off	Easily scratched; does not stain but does show fingerprints	Limited profiles and colours available
Recommended by Mike?	No	Yes	Yes	Yes	Yes	No	Yes	No	No

Tile is a popular choice for back-splashes and a good one. It's durable and offers plenty of styles. To protect the wall behind your tile, you should use a waterproof membrane.

Wherever you install your backsplash, make sure there's a waterproof membrane behind the tile. It's not just behind the sink that water damage can occur.

Paper

There are a number of companies that produce countertops made of paper from managed forests and from 100% recycled post-consumer paper pulp. When the cellulose fibres are combined with natural resins, they form a material that's hard, durable, and resistant to heat and scratches. Finishes can even mimic leather or slate. The cost is comparable to that of granite or engineered stone.

The backsplash

Just about any of the countertop options we've looked at can also be used for the backsplash. Personally, I'd rather see the countertop material used only for the counter, with tile or some other material for the backsplash. Keep the counter flat and level so that it meets the wall at a 90-degree angle. Make sure your contractor finishes the job with a bead of silicone caulking where the counter and wall tile meet, and you won't have to worry about moisture and dirt getting into that crevice.

Tile is the most obvious choice for the backsplash, and there are so many possibilities out there: ceramic, porcelain, marble, glass (including recycled glass), and even metal. Among those options, there's a lot of variety in shape, colour, and finish.

The kitchen floor

Floors account for more surface area than anything else in a home except the walls and ceilings. They set the tone for your whole kitchen, and if you choose well, flooring can add value to your home. Kitchen floors take a lot of wear and tear, so you'll want to choose flooring that can handle it.

But it's not only what you see on top that's important. I've said this before: what's underneath the flooring—the subfloor—is critical to how your floor works, and how long it lasts. The subfloor has to be strong enough to support what you're going to put on top, and it has to be the right material to ensure the finish flooring will adhere properly.

There are a lot of flooring materials to choose from and they vary considerably in price and performance. Before you make your choice, you need to consider your structural needs, looks, durability, and budget, and the product's environmental and health impact.

Ceramic and porcelain tiles

These are still among the most popular kitchen flooring choices. Studies show that tile floors increase a home's resale value more than any other flooring option. And it's no wonder: they're durable, attractive, easy to clean, and available in a wide range of

Ceramic tile floors are great for a kitchen with other high-end finishes.

colours, patterns, and finishes. The latest ceramics do a great job of imitating natural stone but at a much lower cost.

Ceramic tile is made of natural clay-based products, minerals, and water. Glazed ceramic tile resists stains and can be cleaned easily. Depending on the glaze colour, the colour of the ceramic tile body may be visible if the glaze gets scratched. Unglazed tiles are porous and need to be sealed to prevent stains and resist water.

Porcelain tile is also clay-based, but it's fired at extremely high temperatures, making it harder, denser, and more durable than most ceramic tile. Because the colour extends through the thickness of the tile, scratches or chips are less noticeable than in ceramic. And because the material is so dense, you can do tighter grout joints if you want to imitate the look of stone. Porcelain is somewhat more expensive than ceramic tile but it's also very low maintenance. But because porcelain tiles are the same colour throughout, chips and scratches are less noticeable than with ceramic tiles.

The downside of tiles is that they're so hard. This means that most glass objects dropped on a tile floor will shatter, and a large expanse of tile flooring can make for a noisy room because tile doesn't absorb sound. If you're on your feet a lot, tile can be very tiring, and it can be cold underfoot, though radiant in-floor heating can cure that.

Ceramic tile set in a polymer cement may be your best bet in terms of indoor air quality. It's also more durable than tile that's set using adhesives. Ceramic tile has a long life if it's been properly installed, and it biodegrades after removal. Tiles can be reused and may also be crushed and recycled as aggregate material for sidewalks

With proper installation, ceramic is the ideal choice for a kitchen that has access to the outdoors because tile can handle the moisture and dirt that are bound to come in.

and roads. Ceramic and porcelain are my strongest recommendations for kitchen floors. Both types of tile need a strong and level subfloor to prevent cracks in the grout or loose tiles.

Natural stone: Slate, limestone, or marble tiles

Natural stone is probably what most people would choose for their kitchens, if they could afford it. Slate, limestone, and marble are popular but they're also expensive and heavy. And like with all tile floors, a proper subfloor is critical.

Is there a downside to natural stone tiles? Well, they're pricey, that's the first point. They can be cool underfoot, just like ceramic, and while that's okay in the summer, it's another story in the winter. You can make this into an advantage if you use

Linoleum is great when you want a retro choice for your kitchen. The downside is that patterns are limited, and the floor requires regular waxing—maybe not the kind of retro you were looking for.

in-floor heating, either electric or water-based, but again that's an added expense and requires skilled installers. Another disadvantage of natural stone is that it's porous and needs to be sealed every couple of years to prevent staining from everyday use. Acidic fluids such as lemon juice, wine, and vinegar do the most damage.

The other disadvantage to stone is its environmental impact. It's not a renewable resource: once we've taken it out of the ground, we can't make any more of it. As well, the most sought-after kinds of stone—such as granite, marble, sandstone, slate, and limestone—usually need to be transported long distances. Stone doesn't need much processing, but quarrying it, then cutting, polishing, and handling it requires a lot of energy.

Linoleum

You might be surprised to hear this, but linoleum is making a huge comeback. That's probably because it's a great green choice. It's made of wood or cork powder, linseed oil, pine resin, and pigments (for colour), and backed with jute—all of which are natural and renewable resources. It's durable, waterproof, and relatively scuff-resistant, and doesn't burn easily or release harmful pollutants, as some other manufactured floorings do. It's biodegradable once you're done with it—and that could be longer than you own your home because new linoleum has a life of about 40 years. It's also a good choice for people with allergies because it resists dust and bacteria and is easy to clean with very mild cleansers. It does require regular waxing, though, and you might be disappointed by the limited range of patterns.

Vinyl

Vinyl flooring has been big business for years, mainly because it's the cheapest option on the market. The biggest change is probably the number of new designs, textures, and sizes available today. Everything from stone to ceramic to porcelain to wood has been copied to make vinyl floors look as real as possible, all at a very low cost.

Vinyl flooring is available in tiles, planks, and rolls, and can do a good job if what you're looking for is something relatively durable, stain-resistant, and waterproof at an affordable price. The manufacturers say that new vinyl can be laid over old vinyl or linoleum floors if these are in decent shape, but I always recommend taking up the existing floor so you can have a look at the condition of the underlay and replace it if necessary. Some of these older floors, though, may have asbestos in them. Consult with your contractor first so that the material is removed safely.

Some vinyl flooring—like peel-and-stick tile—comes with its own adhesive, though the higher grades need adhesive applied. Some are "click" floors that snap together and "float," without adhesive. The latest innovation is loose-lay vinyl that features an interlayer and "comfort backing" that makes it more comfortable to walk and stand on. The manufacturers promise that it will lie flat and stay flat without the need for glue.

In terms of eco-friendliness, well, there's nothing eco-friendly about it. Because vinyl is basically made from PVC, it's suspected of causing some health issues. The chemicals used to make vinyl products emit hundreds of thousands of pounds of toxic chemicals into the environment each year and very little—less than 1%—of post-consumer PVC, including vinyl flooring, is actually recycled.

Vinyl flooring also smoulders if there's ever a fire in your home and releases corrosive and highly toxic chemicals like hydrogen chloride gas and dioxins. And that's not even mentioning what might be in the adhesives used to install the flooring.

If you're concerned about your home's indoor air quality, or you or members of your family suffer from allergies, then be aware that you'll have to live for a period of time after vinyl flooring has been installed with fumes that could cause you to experience itchy eyes, trouble breathing, and coughing. It's hard to say what the long-term effects might be.

Hardwood may not be the most practical option in a kitchen, but for die-hard wood lovers it may be the only choice.

Hardwood, engineered hardwood, and reclaimed woods

With more and more open-concept homes, there's a trend towards a single type of flooring throughout the main floor of the home, including the kitchen. The choice here is usually wood. But as nice as wood floors are, they're prone to moisture damage from food and water spills, and they can be marked and dented when cans or silverware are dropped on them, or show scratches from your pet's claws. On the plus side, hardwood flooring is somewhat flexible, so the subfloor doesn't need to be as perfectly stable or level as for ceramic tile or other rigid flooring choices.

Like ceramic or stone tile, wood won't harbour allergens, but it's warmer and quieter than hard tiles. With some wood flooring, radiant in-floor heat can be used, but it's a risky option with any woods—especially reclaimed woods—that are prone to a lot of expansion and contraction. Hardwood lasts longer than many other options and can be refinished and restained many times.

Engineered wood is formed by putting together multiple layers of wood, assembled at 90-degree angles to each other to boost stability. The hardwood veneer, usually prefinished, can be resurfaced a number of times, but obviously fewer than real solid hardwood. Engineered wood can be installed as a floating floor—the pieces joined to each other, not to the subfloor—which allows for some movement in winter and summer.

Wood flooring can also be an eco-friendly choice if you buy flooring that has the seal of approval of the Forestry Stewardship Council (FSC), ensuring the wood planks come from forests harvested in a sustainable manner. Engineered wood cuts down on waste and cost because it has a composite core under a thin layer of wood. Some producers claim they get as much as five times the square footage out of the log compared with traditionally manufactured wood flooring. Recycled flooring salvaged from old barns and warehouses and remilled for home use is another green option.

Laminates

Today's manufacturing technologies allow laminate tiles to imitate a wide range of materials with amazing accuracy, so you can have the look of hardwood, stone, or ceramic tile for lower cost and less maintenance. Laminate floors are made of an inner core of pressed and glued wood material with a photographic image laminated on the surface. While they're extremely impact- and scratch-resistant, they *can* be scratched, and can be damaged by prolonged exposure to moisture.

Laminate flooring has achieved great popularity in recent years because of how easily it can be installed and because of its low cost—about one-third the price of true hardwood. But if the cost seems ridiculously low, the quality may be low as well.

And let's face it: laminate is not the real thing, and it's not a good choice for high-moisture areas like kitchens.

Bamboo

Bamboo is becoming a popular alternative to hardwood and has almost become the flooring of choice for its eco-friendliness. Not a wood at all but a grass, bamboo is a fast-growing, renewable resource.

On the downside, most bamboo flooring comes from the Asia-Pacific region, particularly China and Vietnam, which means it takes a lot of energy to transport it to North America. Adhesives used in bamboo flooring sometimes contain a urea formaldehyde resin, although products that contain minimal or no formaldehyde are available for a higher price. In the manufacturing process, bamboo is steamed under pressure and/or boiled to remove natural sugars and impurities, then kiln-dried and milled, and finally the strips are joined together with glue, heat, and pressure. The result is a product that is hard and rigid, a lot like wood.

Bamboo floors are also installed and maintained in the same manner as hardwood floors, and like wood floors they're available in both solid strips and engineered strips (several plies laminated together). Like wood, bamboo is prone to moisture damage and may not be an ideal choice for kitchens. A lot depends on the sealant, and it's worth going to a high-grade bamboo if you're planning to use it in the kitchen.

Cork

Cork is marketed as one of the ultimate green flooring choices, and it's not hard to see why. It's highly renewable (though at a lower rate than bamboo), and even "virgin" cork is harvested sustainably from several Mediterranean countries.

Some manufacturers claim their cork flooring is hypoallergenic. All-natural cork flooring is preferable to cork-vinyl composites that have a PVC backing. In the past, urea formaldehyde was used to bind cork granules into flooring, but that was phased out in the 1980s. Today, urea melamine, phenol formaldehyde, and natural proteins are used as binders instead, which has reduced VOC problems.

Techniques for installing cork planks or tiles vary from nailing to gluing. If gluing is required, I recommend that you choose low-VOC adhesives. Tiles will need to be sealed, and again I recommend a low-VOC polyurethane sealer or a natural wax.

Cork floor keeps its shape well and is naturally mould-, moisture-, and rot-resistant and can sometimes "self-heal" if it's dented. As durable as hardwood flooring (and comparable in cost), biodegradable, and non-toxic, cork can even be ground up for compost. It absorbs sound and pressure, which makes it comfortable and less tiring to walk on than some harder types of flooring.

Bamboo is a grass, not a wood, so in manufacturing bamboo floors, the grass is boiled, then kiln-dried to help harden it. Bamboo is then cut into strips and glued together for flooring.

Concrete

If you like the industrial loft look, you may be considering concrete flooring. But it's not a practical choice for most home renovations because it's so heavy. Because of the minimal depth required to pour a solid concrete floor that won't crack or crumble, and because of the joist strength required to support the additional weight, concrete is usually not an option when you're renovating an existing house. Loft buildings, which are usually made of reinforced concrete rather than wood, are still the most likely place to find concrete floors. If you're starting from scratch on a house, you can make the structure strong enough to handle concrete, and you can get radiant in-floor heat, which is a fantastic form of heat, installed at the same time. The concrete can be finished with a variety of stains or acid etchings that make it look more interesting and less like a warehouse floor. But keep in mind that concrete is generally hard on the feet if you're standing on it for long stretches, which is likely to be the case in kitchens. It's fantastic, though, for passive solar heat gain and for radiant heat, which makes it a sustainable choice.

Rubber

A flooring look that's crossed over from industrial kitchens, rubber is comfortable to stand on, although there isn't a huge choice in colour or pattern. It's relatively expensive and difficult to keep really clean.

Virgin rubber is manufactured from latex, the sap of rubber trees, which grow in tropical areas. Asia provides most of the world's natural rubber, meaning a big carbon footprint to import it, although it can also be produced synthetically. Several varieties of rubber flooring are made from recycled materials, typically rubber tires, meaning that there are abundant raw materials in North America, to say the least. Recycled rubber flooring is generally less expensive and more durable than virgin flooring. Rubber flooring is usually flammable and some people are allergic to it.

Carpet

Wall-to-wall carpeting doesn't belong in the kitchen. The kitchen floor needs to be easy to clean and carpeting just gets too embedded with dirt, stains, and grime. That said, small area rugs could work in areas where you'll spend a fair amount of time standing (such as in front of the sink) and want a little cushioning, but make sure to use proper skid-resistant underpads to prevent tripping.

Kitchen floors at a glance

Material	Ceramic or porcelain tile	Natural stone: Slate, limestone, or marble tile	Linoleum	Vinyl	Cork	Hardwood
Durability	Extremely durable	Extremely durable	Very durable	Depends on grade	Fairly durable	Fairly durable
Water-resistance	High	High	High	High	High	Low to moderate
Range of colours/ patterns	Almost unlimited	Limited to natural colours	Broad	Broad	Broad range of stain colours; patterns can be created	Broad range of stain colours; patterns can be created
Cost	Moderate to high	Moderate to high	Moderate	Low to moderate	Moderate to high	Moderate to high
Environmental concerns	Uses renewable resources; energy requirements to produce ceramic tile are high	Uses natural but non-renewable products; may be transported over long distances	Uses non-toxic, renewable resources; dry cleaning recommended, reducing waste water; biodegradable	Manufacturing process is not environmentally friendly; will off-gas harmful chemicals in the home	Uses bark rather than whole trees; may be transported over long distances	Uses natural and renewable resources (FSC rating)
Good to know	Subfloor prep is key, and grout must be sealed	Subfloor prep is key, and grout must be sealed, and floor sealed yearly	Easy on joints for long periods of standing; resists dust and bacteria	Mastics are prone to mould	Naturally repels water and insects; resists mould; must be sealed	Can be dented and scratched by normal kitchen use
Recommended by Mike for kitchen use?	Yes	Yes	No	No	Yes	No

Engineered hardwood	Laminates (click flooring)	Bamboo	Concrete	Rubber	Carpet	Mesquite
Fairly durable	Somewhat durable	Fairly durable	Extremely durable	Extremely durable	Depends on grade	Extremely durable
Low to moderate	Low to moderate	Low to moderate	High	High	Low	Low to moderate
Broad range of stain colours; patterns can be created	Broad	Broad range of stain colours; patterns can be created	Can be stained or painted	Limited	Broad range of colours only	Broad range of colours and patterns
Moderate to high	Low to moderate	Moderate to high	Low to moderate	Moderate to high	Low to moderate	Moderate to high
Uses some natural and renewable resources	Manufacturing process is not environmentally friendly	Uses a fast-growing, renewable resource; may be transported over long distances	Uses natural materials or post-industrial recycled	Manufacturing process is not environmentally friendly; some recycled rubber flooring available	Manufacturing process is not environmentally friendly; carpet will off-gas in first months after installation	Uses fast-growing renewable resource; produced in North America
Can be dented and scratched by normal kitchen use	Warranty may be void if used in wet area such as kitchen	Installs much like hardwood	Prone to cracking; must be sealed yearly	Hard to keep clean	Hard to keep clean in wet areas	Minimal shrinkage
No	No	No	No	No	No	Yes

Following up: Checklist

You've got a lot of information now about the choices you can make for your new kitchen. Use the following checklist to keep track of your decisions.

Layout

Basic layout description: _____

Checked against layout "rules" for good design and operation? _____

Cabinetry

Custom or stock?_____

Material and finish: _____

Product name/number:_____

Special features: _____

Lighting

(show placement of all light fixtures on drawing)

Type and number of fixtures for general lighting: _____

Product name/number:_____

Type and number of fixtures for task lighting: _____

Product name/number:_____

Type and number of fixtures for accent lighting: _____

Product name/number:_____

Other electrical needs

Number of outlets (show placement on drawing):_____

Appliances needing dedicated outlets: _____

Electric range? _____

Other wiring needed for telephone, cable, Internet access: _____

Type of range hood: _____

Product name/number for range hood: _____

Ceiling fan(s): _____

Product name/number of ceiling fan(s): _____

Three-way switches required (show locations on drawing): _____

Kitchen island?_____

Number of outlets in island (show locations on drawing): _____

Electrical in-floor heat?_____

Plumbing fixtures

Type and material of main sink (show location on drawing): _____

Product name/number of main sink: _____

Product name/number of faucet for main sink: _____

Type and material of secondary sink (show location on drawing): _____

Product name/number of secondary sink: _____

Product name/number of faucet for secondary sink: _____

Special features (e.g., pot-filler over stove): _____

Appliances

Product name/number of range: _____

Product name/number of refrigerator: _____

Product name/number of microwave: _____

Additional appliances? _____

Product names/numbers of any additional appliances: _____

Countertops and backsplash

Type of countertop: _____

Total square footage: _____

Nosing profile: _____

Product name/number/colour: _____

Backsplash type (if different from countertop): _____

Product name/number/colour of backsplash: _____

Flooring

Type of flooring: _____

Total square footage: _____

Product name/number/colour: _____

CHAPTER 6

Creating the Just-Right Bathroom

Bathroom design can be as wide open as your imagination. If you're lucky, and you've got two or more bathrooms in your house, you can tailor each one to its specific use and to the people who use it. Each type of bathroom—family bathroom, powder room, ensuite bathroom, guest bathroom—needs to be carefully planned. Just like in your kitchen, that means you've got a lot of choices ahead of you.

But along with the design of your bathroom, you've got to think about the fact that every bathroom is a "wet zone"—and your contractor needs to know how to handle this properly. In fact, everything we do as we renovate a bathroom should ultimately be about keeping the water from damaging our homes. There are several reasons for this.

First, there's the lifespan of your bathroom. Using better construction methods means you're going to have a new bathroom that lasts much longer. Isn't it worth spending the money from the start to get a better product that will last longer?

Second, there's mould. When water continually or repeatedly gets into places where it doesn't belong—under the finished floor, for example, or behind the tiles, or under the lip of your drop-in sink—you're going to get mould. (If it dries out, and if it's once or twice, it'll be fine.) Mould is bad for your health, especially for children, older people, and anyone with a weakened immune system. It can make respiratory difficulties such as asthma worse, and can cause allergic reactions as well as ear, nose, and throat irritations.

Finally, excess moisture and mould will cause decay and rot in your home. We're not just talking about a little bit of mildew on the caulking; this is about rot that goes right into the wall studs and the floor joists. When you keep water and moisture away from framing members, you don't have to worry about rot and long-term damage to the structure. Building properly helps us avoid the problems that come with water damage and mould.

The better way to build a bathroom

So what does "building properly" mean? For me, there are a few absolute standards that should be set when you're working on a bathroom.

Spend the money on watertight systems for the floor, shower, and tub area. These will ensure a seamless system of waterproofing membranes under your finished flooring and plumbing fixtures, behind wall tiles, and around your shower drain. I can't say enough how important it is to make the shower area absolutely watertight, and there are products available that provide a number of different layers, and products that will ensure your shower stall never leaks into the surrounding framing or flooring. Invest in this system and your bathroom will last at least twice as long.

Invest in insulation to prevent heat loss (or gain) on exterior walls, to protect your plumbing from freezing. A closed-cell polyurethane foam insulation on the exterior walls, called Walltite Eco, is the best you can buy. Sound insulation batts, or special sound-insulating drywall, are available for interior walls. Make sure the sound-insulating drywall is installed on the outside of the bathroom wall, since it's not a mould-resistant product.

Use only mould-resistant products in the bathroom. For walls around bathtubs and showers, that means cement board only. Never use green drywall in the shower or bathtub area. For other parts of the bathroom, use a mould-resistant drywall by Georgia Pacific.

Make sure your toilet is installed using a wax gasket, not the old-fashioned rubber kind. Wax won't absorb moisture the way rubber does, so it can't lead to mould and moisture damage to the wooden subfloor under the toilet.

Another way to fight mould is to use only silicone caulking—not latex—in the bathroom. Make sure you get the mould- and mildew-resistant type, or you'll see mould growing on the caulking eventually. Use it for the corners of your shower, over the grout lines in the corners if you're using tiles, and around a custom shower to make it waterproof and to make the glass adhere to the wall. Silicone caulking should also be used around the lip of the sink, and in a thin bead around the faucet. These extra measures are good insurance against water getting into places that it doesn't belong.

Using a wax gasket, rather than rubber, when installing your toilet is the better way to help prevent leaks.

Never cover up a problem. There are a lot of companies out there trying to sell a "bathroom in a day" type of deal. They come in and cover up your old bathtub and old tile walls with a one-piece acrylic product, and some companies offer a similar service with countertops. What a terrible way to spend your money. If your old tub and tiles are in such bad shape that they need to be replaced, don't you think you should remove the worn-out, water-damaged materials first and fix the problem at the source? Always go to the source by tearing out old, and starting fresh.

Just gut it!

I hear a lot of people say that they want to do a simple or quick reno on their bathroom. They don't want to disturb the plumbing too much, and they want to keep the fixtures if they possibly can. Often they don't want to replace the tub because it will be "too much trouble" and it will cost too much.

Is it always necessary to gut your bathroom to do the job right? Well, let me put it this way: I have rarely gone into a bathroom to do a reno without having to gut it and start over again. I've done so many bathrooms over the years, and what I've found most often is that one reno gets done over top of the last one, and so on. You end up with layers of cover-up, and that's not good. How can you tell what's under the floor and behind the walls if you don't take it apart? How can you tell if the plumbing is still working properly and not leaking? It's true that most leaks will show up somewhere—say, on the flooring, around the toilet, or maybe on the ceiling of the room below—but not always. I've seen situations where the previous contractor left so much rubble and crap in the floor cavity that the dripping water was being absorbed by the garbage and so the leaks weren't showing up. But believe me, the leaks were there, and it took a lot of tear-out—of ceilings, walls, and floors—to get to the problem and fix it.

Don't spend any money on a reno that doesn't fix all the problems. The only way you'll know if there are problems is to do a complete gut of the room. Take it right back to the studs and the floor joists and see what the plumbing looks like—the supply lines, the stack, the venting, everything. See what the wiring is like. I once took apart a half-finished shower stall and found a hidden junction box on the wall next to the plumbing. Water and electricity—the perfect combination for a disaster.

The other thing you'll know if you gut the bathroom is whether there's any water damage behind the walls. If there was a leak previously, or an ongoing leak, there can be a lot of damage that you can't see. You'll probably need to replace drywall and maybe even framing, but there are two advantages to this. One, you'll know that you've taken care of any situations that might be producing mould, which is so unhealthy

to have in your home. Two, you'll have the chance to replace that old drywall with cement board around any wet areas. That's the best you can get for the bathroom, and I absolutely recommend it. Use a waterproofing system over the walls and floor of the shower and tub area before you tile, and you'll have the most watertight bathroom you've ever seen. That's how to do it right, and how to spend your money right.

One more real advantage to gutting the bathroom? The chance to design the room exactly as you want it. It's a lot easier to change the position of fixtures and plumbing once the walls are open and everything is exposed. Don't look at gutting as a problem: it's an opportunity to do the job right.

Planning the layout

A bathroom that works well and looks good has probably been designed. That means that someone—you, the contractor, a designer, maybe all three—has thought about who's going to use the room, and how, and what the best choices are, and they've planned for everything. Doing this should be one of your first steps. Here are some basic questions to guide your thinking.

Who is the bathroom for?

The bathroom you're renovating might be for the whole family to use, for the master bedroom only, or for guests only. If it's the only bathroom in the house, it has to function well for every person who lives in the house, and visitors too. The needs of every person using the bathroom have to be taken into account. A small child has different needs than a teenager, a senior, or a person in a wheelchair. Keep in mind that the more people who use the bathroom, the more storage you're likely to need as well, for toiletries, medications, clean towels, dirty laundry, extra toilet paper, etc.

What is most convenient for the people using the bathroom?

Access and privacy should be at the top of your list. A powder room should be accessible to the living areas, but shouldn't open directly into the living room, dining room, or kitchen. Ideally, a powder room will open into a hallway or some other "transitional area" where users feel they can enter and leave the bathroom without drawing attention to themselves. A powder room should be located on the level of the house where guests are most likely to spend time.

An ensuite (or master) bathroom adjoins the master bedroom, so it's usually meant for two people. It's best if it's large enough for both people to use at the same time. Double sinks and/or separate sections of cabinetry and counter space can provide personal space for each person. A separate shower and tub are ideal. For those who like a lot of privacy, consider putting the toilet in its own "closet."

Bathtubs and showers should be fitted with grab bars, no matter how young or old the users of the bathroom might be.

What is safest for those who use the bathroom?

Safety is an issue in any bathroom, because of the possibility of slipping and falling on wet surfaces. Think about safety when you choose flooring—it should be as non-slippery as possible. There are lots of unglazed, non-slip tile options out there, which would be my recommendation. Bathtubs and showers should be fitted with grab bars and floor mats, no matter how young or old the users of the bathroom might be. If you don't want to install the grab bars until later in life when you need them, have the framing built in now so it can be used later. Make a drawing of the framing with exact measurements so you'll know where to anchor the grab bar in the future, and take pictures of the framing before the wall board goes up.

What do you want?

A big impetus for renovating a bathroom is the chance to get it exactly the way you want it. You want it to function efficiently and you want it to look great. Take this opportunity to think about luxury upgrades such as heated towel racks, multiple shower heads, or a bathtub with jets for relaxation. And don't forget about storage. Most of us have more toiletries, towels, and small appliances than we think. Building sufficient storage will keep your newly renovated bathroom from looking cluttered and messy.

How can you get what you want with the space you have?

Let's face it: most of us are working with space restrictions. Sometimes you have to settle for less than you'd like. In most cases, though, if you keep trying to come up with the right layout, you can have what you want, or most of it. The key is to have an open mind, and not commit yourself to the first design that pops up in your head.

My suggestion? Get out the graph paper, take careful measurements of the room, and plot them onto your paper, then start making diagrams of the various possibilities. Make sure each drawing shows the exact placement of windows (unless you're willing to change them) and the vent stack (which will determine the position of the toilet unless you're willing to go to the expense of moving or adding vent lines to the stack). The bathtub should probably stay in the same location, unless you're prepared to do structural work if you move it, which will mean removing the floor boards to beef up the joists underneath. I like to see the bathroom door open into the room, preferably right against a wall. This is the best use of space. Use the design "rules" listed on page 159 to make sure you leave enough room for each fixture.

Give yourself a number of days (or longer) to decide on a design, since more ideas will come to you once you start thinking about it. And always, always ask for suggestions from your contractor, who has probably seen a lot of bathrooms and will have some good ideas. Hire a bathroom designer as well, if you don't feel up to the task of designing the space yourself. (For more on how to hire a designer for your bathroom or kitchen, see page 97.)

MIKE'S TIP

Steam baths

You may be thinking about a steam bath, a sauna, or even a hot tub in your bathroom. Don't put these in your house—if you want a full spa, go to one. This much moisture in one room or house will be trouble.

This bathroom looks great, but I'd like to see some grab bars in the shower and bath area for safety. I hope the tiles are textured to prevent slipping.

Layout basics for every bathroom

Just as there are design "rules" for kitchen layout, there are also rules for how to position bathroom fixtures in the most safe, comfortable, and efficient ways.

Here are a few things to know:

1. A standard bathtub is 60 inches by 32 inches. Allow an "activity area" in front of it that's at least 44 inches by 28 inches for accessibility.

2. A standard washstand (sink set into a vanity, or pedestal sink) is about 28 inches wide and 24 inches deep. You can adjust the height of the vanity if you want (or any of the dimensions) if you're having the cabinetry custom-fit or customized by a carpenter. Allow a minimum activity area of 40 inches by 28 inches in front of the washstand for clearance.

3. A double vanity needs a minimum of 60 inches in length.

4. Allow a minimum space of 32 inches by 48 inches for the toilet and the area in front of it.

5. If you're planning on a bidet, allow a space that's the same size as you allow for the toilet: 32 inches by 48 inches.

6. A walk-in shower stall needs to be at least 32 inches by 32 inches, but 36 inches is more comfortable. The minimum height for a shower head to be set is 80 inches—but set it higher if people in your house are taller than average. Allow an activity area of 28 inches by 36 inches in front of the shower.

A whirlpool tub, when it's full of water, can weigh over 600 pounds even before you get in. If you're planning on adding one, make sure the structure of your house can support it.

Beyond design: How plumbing and structure affect your bathroom choices

Here's something else that's important to know when you're planning a bathroom: there are plumbing and structural issues when you change the layout of your bathroom.

First, you'll usually pay more for plumbing if you reconfigure the elements in your bathroom. Moving everything around will mean a lot of extra time for your plumber. Remember that labour is a substantial part (about half) of the overall plumbing cost, with materials making up the rest. But if you're dealing with older plumbing that needs to be replaced anyway, you probably won't see much of a spike in costs, and any cost will be worth it to get the layout you want.

Second, the toilet has to be located within 5 feet of the main vent stack. As long as the toilet is within 5 feet of the stack, it can be vented directly through the stack, and you should have enough air behind water for a good, strong flush. If the toilet is farther than 5 feet from the stack, the vent line will need to be extended, or you'll need a separate air line to the stack. The plumbing code has specific rules about venting angles and runs, and your contractor should know about them. Never let a contractor talk you into using a "cheater valve" so you can put the toilet just about anywhere. It's almost never allowed for a toilet because it just doesn't allow enough air into the system to really work. If you've got a permit—and I know you will, because it's always necessary for bathroom renos—the plumbing inspector will make sure that everything is done to code during the rough-in stage.

Third, you've got to be aware that a tub full of water weighs an awful lot. It has to be adequately supported from underneath, so make sure your contractor checks your framing, especially if you're moving the tub to a different location in the bathroom. Cast iron tubs, whirlpools, soaking tubs, and sunken tubs often require more support than traditional, lower-grade (lighter) tubs. Just think about it: if a gallon of water weighs about 8 pounds, and an average bathtub holds about 80 gallons, you're looking at 640 pounds before anyone even gets in! Then you add about 120 to 180 pounds (or more, if you're a hockey player or a contractor), and you're looking at a really hefty load on your floor—about the same weight as your average grand piano.

Most floors today are built with 2 × 8 joists—that's the minimum code requirement. And those 2 × 8s are actually 1½ × 7½s, which is just enough to keep your floor from falling in, but that's about it. When you substantially increase the weight load with a much bigger tub, you could get cracks in the tile, possibly in the drywall too, and water may begin to penetrate the structure through those cracks.

So, to support the extra load, your contractor should be pulling up the floorboards to expose the joists, and laminating new 2 × 8s alongside the existing joists. Ideally, the new 2 × 8s will run the entire length of the existing ones, but that may not be possible; whatever can be added is better than nothing. The new boards should be glued and screwed to the old ones, and even bolted together if you have to add as many as three extra boards for strength. That horizontal load also needs to be picked up by vertical points.

Your bathroom can affect your resale value

Bathrooms can be a huge selling feature when you put your house on the market. But an outdated, unattractive, or badly renovated bathroom can also take a bite out of your selling price. Even though I'm a big believer in making your house into the home that you want to live in, not building and renovating for the next person, I think it's smart to put your reno dollars into a bathroom that will help you when you have to sell. The first thing to do is make sure you get a quality reno done. The second thing is to avoid making changes that will make your house a tough sell.

Here are a few things that might fall into the "what to avoid" category:

1. **Unusual colours for fixtures such as toilets or bathtubs.** Stick to neutral colours such as white or ivory for these expensive-to-change fixtures, since a homebuyer might be turned off by black or aqua. Express yourself with colour on stuff that can be easily changed, such as your walls or towels.

2. **A family bathroom without a bathtub.** If you're one of those people who prefers showers and never takes baths, you might be tempted not to waste space on a bathtub. That may be fine for a small master bathroom, but not for a family bathroom—especially if it's the only bathroom in the house. Most prospective homebuyers want a "normal" bathroom with a tub, and will walk away from a house that doesn't have this bathroom basic.

3. **A master bedroom and bathroom that are combined, without any walls to separate the two rooms.** You may think this is a great arrangement, but many others won't. If you're determined to have the openness, at least put the toilet in a separate "closet" or small room of its own.

4. **Windows that rob you of privacy.** Natural light is great, but not if it means everyone can see you at your most private times of the day or night. Use etched or pebbled glass for privacy, or place windows higher on the wall than you would elsewhere in the house. That massive tub set into a bay window might be practical if you live in the middle of nowhere—but that's not the case for most people. Be prepared to install window coverings.

Cabinetry

A lot of your cabinetry choices will probably boil down to this: will you go with stock cabinets or custom? You'll pay up to three times more for custom cabinetry, but you'll get the highest quality, and you should be able to get exactly what you want. It can be worth the extra cost, especially when you're trying to make the most efficient use of a small space.

There's another reason you should consider higher-end cabinets in the bathroom. The bathroom is a wet zone—always remember this—so any products you install have to be able to withstand moisture. If you buy cabinets with a pressboard core, those cabinets are going to wick up the moisture in no time, and then you'll be right back where you started: renovating your bathroom (or at least replacing an important part of it). Go for solid wood if you possibly can afford it, and make sure it has many layers of a good, waterproof finish.

To find out more about cabinetry, and how you can tell good stock cabinets from ones that are just so-so, see the kitchen section on page 106.

Rather than use either custom or stock cabinets, you might choose a different route. For a number of years now, furniture has been taking over the bathroom. Everyone started looking for the perfect antique chest of drawers or table to turn into a vanity, and getting their plumber to drop in a sink or set a vessel sink on top. Eventually, manufacturers caught on and started producing vanities that mimic the look of antique furniture. The freestanding vanity came into being (well, came back into being—you've probably seen those old-style washstands with basins and pitchers of water), and has moved beyond the antique look into more contemporary styles as well. Now these manufactured pieces are just another type of stock cabinetry.

Converting a piece of furniture into a vanity can be a great look, but think about the damage that water can do to wood (especially the old, dry wood of an antique), and protect your wood accordingly, with many layers of an oil-based polyurethane. You could have a countertop of solid-surface material, granite, or marble, fitted for the top as well, which would look fantastic and keep water from coming into contact with wood. Just remember to seal any natural stone product that you might use, and keep resealing it on a regular basis.

One more thing about using old furniture, especially a table, as a washstand: you might end up with some plumbing exposed, and your plumber will need to know about that in advance. You'll want your plumber to use chrome, nickel, or copper fittings under the sink, rather than plastic, and it's possible they'll need to order those in well before the installation date.

Make sure your contractor knows early if you're planning to modify antique furniture so there's time for the plumber to work with it.

Lighting

Just like in your kitchen or any other room, a good lighting plan in the bathroom uses a variety of different types of lighting.

Start with general or ambient lighting. The goal is a room with a comfortable level of brightness without any glare. The most popular source of general light for the bathroom is a flush or semi-flush ceiling fixture. We're also seeing a lot more pendant fixtures (like you might use over an island) or even mini-chandeliers in the bathroom, but avoid hanging these over bathtubs. Ambient lights need to be placed in the centre of the bathroom so that the light is spread out evenly.

There's a rule of thumb for figuring out how much general lighting you need: multiply the length and width of the bathroom—for instance, 10 feet by 10 feet—then multiply that by a factor of 1.5. So, in this example, you would need 150 watts of general light as your first layer.

Next comes good task lighting. It's probably the most important lighting in the bathroom. The most common mistake people make is putting recessed ceiling fixtures

A tubular skylight can add natural light to your bathroom.

directly over the mirror. These cast shadows on the face, making shaving and applying makeup difficult—not to mention the fact that you won't like how you look in bad lighting. Vertical fixtures or sconces mounted on either side of the mirror are best for casting even light across the face. The ideal is one sconce on each side of the mirror, about 5½ to 6½ feet from the ground. Sconces or vertical bars should be separated by a distance of 28 inches or more.

With the size and positioning of some vanity mirrors, sidelights can be impossible and you have to put the light fixture over the mirror. In that case it should be placed 75 to 80 inches above the floor and, like all vanity lighting, contain at least 150 watts—ideally spread over a fixture that's at least 24 inches long so that the light will spread out evenly on the person standing in front of the mirror. Calculating the amount of task lighting you need is similar to the previous example; the only difference is you multiply by a factor of 2.5. So for a bathroom that's 10 feet by 10 feet, you need about 250 watts of task lighting.

Don't overlook lighting in the shower or bathtub. One or two recessed lights in each of these areas can make a big difference to your comfort and safety level. Your electrician will need to use the low-voltage recessed lights that are designed with special waterproof housings and are rated for use in wet zones.

Dimmers make good sense in the bathroom because they give you absolute control over the amount of light. In a very small space like a powder room, having a dimmer on the vanity fixture might even provide all-in-one lighting: task, ambient, and accent. Dimmers also conserve energy. The total savings depends on how much you dim the bulb, but one dimmed just 10% will last twice as long as a bulb at full brightness. And, of course, installing LED fixtures and bulbs wherever possible will also save you a lot of money over time.

Other electrical needs in the bathroom

Before you assume that your electrical contractor will "just know" how to wire your bathroom, you need to make some decisions and then convey your choices in writing. Planning for electrical, along with your lighting, is actually a big part of the overall bathroom design. Make sure you have answers to the following questions, and put it all together in a drawing and written plan for your general contractor and electrical contractor.

How many outlets do you need, and where?

Consider the height of cabinets that you plan to use, especially if you're thinking of going with cabinets that are higher than standard, since this will affect the placement of outlets and your electrician will need to know this ahead of time. Make sure you request enough outlets in the vanity area, and check that your electrician will be using GFCI outlets for any outlet within 3 feet of a water source.

What type of fan will you have installed?

Fans are often sold in combination with a light fixture, and you need to make sure that both the fan and the light are the right size and strength for your bathroom. Don't cheap out here. The minimum code requirement is a standard 90-CFM fan, but I don't think that's enough. To get a fan that actually moves the moist air out of the room, you need something that's at least 150-CFM. I like the higher-end fans made by Panasonic, which move the air efficiently and quietly. You won't regret the expense. Make sure your electrician knows that you want the fan and light to operate on separate switches. The fan should be switched separately so you can leave it running after your shower is done, without having to leave the light on as well.

Will your bathroom have a bathtub with jets?

These require additional power, which should be kept in mind when considering how large a service panel you'll need.

Do you want heat lamps in the bathroom?

Heat lamps are an inexpensive way of adding some heat to the bathroom, but it takes a while for them to make a difference to the room temperature, and especially to heat those tile floors. A better, but more expensive, solution to cold floors is in-floor heat.

Will you splurge on in-floor radiant heat in the bathroom?

It can be done either with a hydronic system or an electric mat system, but for one room only (the bathroom) I recommend the electrical system. This is one of the best upgrades because you can have floors that are always warm. Your general contractor and electrician need to know that you're planning to use in-floor heat so they can provide the necessary wiring. It has to be wired directly to the electrical panel, not tied into any existing wiring. The product I recommend, Nuheat, comes in standard sizes or can be custom fit to your bathroom, since the mat in which the wires are run can't be cut after manufacture.

Your final drawing—whether done by you or by a licensed designer or architect—should show the location (including distance from the floor) of every outlet and light fixture.

Plumbing

The bathroom is a wet zone, so it's obvious that the real guts of the room are based on water: water coming in; water and waste going out. Because there's such a range of quality out there, you've got some tough choices to make around faucets, tubs, showers, and toilets. In general, you get what you pay for in plumbing. I always recommend going with higher-quality plumbing products and fixtures because you'll have a superior bathroom in the end, and you'll be less likely to have leaks and other problems in the future. Spend a little more now and you'll have a headache-free bathroom for years.

Here are a few things I recommend as must-haves for the bathroom:

1. **Proper venting for every fixture.** The principle of air-behind-water is what plumbing is all about. If there's no air—or not enough air—coming into your system, your fixtures won't work the way they should. If I see water draining slowly from a sink or tub, or I don't see a whirlpool in the toilet when it flushes, I know there are venting problems. You don't know what proper venting looks like, but a licensed plumber does. Make sure your contractor hires only a licensed plumber to work on your house. And go the extra mile and make sure your job starts with gutting the bathroom right to the floor joists. All the existing plumbing will be exposed, and your plumber will have easy access to make changes the right way. This is the best way to ensure that your fixtures are installed and vented properly.

2. **Shut-offs for the supply lines to every sink and toilet.** The building and plumbing codes don't require this, but it's something you can ask your contractor for, and you should. Just imagine that you've got water pouring out of a supply line under your sink and you've got to run down to the basement to the main water shut-off. In an emergency, you can easily shut off any fixture if they have individual controls. Make sure your contractor doesn't use compression-fitting shut-offs, though; ask for the single-lever ball valves instead. They're more expensive, but they'll perform much better over time.

3. **A pressure-balanced shower control.** For your comfort and safety, you want to avoid those moments when the shower suddenly goes from warm to scalding because someone else in the house has opened a tap or flushed a toilet. For a slightly higher price, get a pressure-balanced shower control that will eliminate those moments.

4. **Ventilation, ventilation, ventilation.** I can't say this often enough: your house needs to breathe, and you need to get that moist air out of your house.

We produce so much moisture in a day: cooking, breathing, and of course showering and bathing. That moisture has to be moved out, or it's going to create problems with the materials in our homes. Protect your investment and create a healthy environment in your home by having an operable bathroom window (if at all possible), and a high-quality fan that moves at least 150 cubic feet of air per minute (150 CFM). That fan will not only remove moisture and odours, it will even take away some contaminants, such as off-gases from building materials, dust mites, mould, etc. It's worth the expense to buy a good one.

Faucets and shower heads

Think about how many faucets the average bathroom has: one if it's a powder room, but for the average bathroom it's probably three or more—the sink, shower, bath, and maybe even a bidet. That's a lot. The common denominator is that they all carry water. Choosing faucets that are high quality, especially with eco-friendly features, can save you water and a lot of money over time.

Whatever style of faucet you choose, the ones with ceramic disks to control water flow are the best quality.

Let's start with the sink faucet. Begin by thinking about the type of handle you want for your faucet. You can choose from single-handle or two-handle. Many sinks are pre-drilled for either a two-handle or single-handle faucet, but in some cases you can get the holes drilled for the specific faucet you want.

When installing a top-mounted sink, be sure that a bead of caulking is run along the outer lip edge to help prevent water from seeping under the sink.

There are three basic faucet styles including single-hole, widespread, and centre-set models. The single-hole style has only one spout and handle from which the water temperature and flow are controlled. Centre-set faucets come with either single-handle or double-handle controls. They're also commonly called 4"-spread or 4"-centre faucets because they're mostly used in a three-hole basin, with the outer holes measuring 4 inches from the centre. The industry standard for bathroom faucet inlet holes is 4 inches apart, although as bathrooms and bathroom fixtures have increased in size, some faucets now have holes as much as 8 inches from the centre, which is why they're called widespread.

Choose the right sink for the space.

Bathroom sinks come in all shapes and sizes. You can get drop-in sinks, under-mount sinks, pedestal sinks, vessel sinks—you name it, it's out there.

For really tight spaces in powder rooms, there are lots of very small sinks available now. You could use a corner model, or a narrow sink that gives you just enough room to wash your hands. But don't use these small sinks in a family bathroom that receives a lot of use—they just wouldn't be practical.

Vessel sinks, which look like a bowl, sit on top of the counter and need a faucet with a higher spout in order to reach the sink comfortably. This type of sink can also use a wall-mounted faucet. Remember that the greater the distance the water travels before reaching the bowl, the more splashing there will be. Make sure the faucet is installed so the water flows into the middle of the sink. (For more on what to look for in faucets and faucet mechanisms, see the kitchen section on page 121.)

In the shower, the single-handle bath and shower faucet is the simplest choice because it adjusts pressure and heat with one motion. There are specialized whirl-pool faucets that include single-handle and double-handle versions.

You can get creative if you've got the room and the budget for a stand-alone shower (separate from the bathtub). There are all kinds of options, from shower heads that offer multiple settings to gentle downpours to vertical spas offering full-body jets. You can even install a waterfall shower head (sometimes called a rainshower head), if you're looking for luxury. Keep in mind that these will use more water than a low-flow or even a conventional shower head.

A low-flow shower head can reduce the amount of water you use by 50% over standard models, and the newest versions won't affect your water pressure. Some are aided by small turbine-like mechanisms that spin the water for a more forceful spray. Some new models have self-cleaning systems that make them more resistant to mineral and lime buildup.

The toilet

What's the most important feature in the bathroom? Your toilet—something you might not care too much about until it's not working properly. On a daily basis, what you really want is a toilet that flushes well—every time, the first time.

Don't pay attention to just how a toilet looks. Inside the toilet is what really counts when you're picking one. A well-designed toilet with a wide throat opening gives you a stronger flush and fewer clogs.

The old standard in toilets used a lot of water—20 litres. In the early 1990s the first "water saver" toilets became available with a 13-litre flush, and they're still available. In 1996, the Ontario Building Code began requiring 6-litre toilets for all new homes, but so far Ontario is the only province to have this type of regulation.

Some of those first-generation 6-litre toilets didn't work very well, but most of today's models have been re-engineered to flush better. Still, you'll sometimes find that an ultra-low-flush toilet takes two or three flushes to work properly. That could be a problem with the installation: if there isn't enough airflow behind water because of inadequate venting, you'll always have problems with flushing. But sometimes it's the design itself. The key is to find a toilet with a wide throat opening—it's definitely got to be bigger than the standard 1¾ inches. The bigger the opening, the stronger the flush you're going to get.

There are various technologies in toilets. Gravity-type toilets are what you'll find in most homes, and what you'll probably find at the big-box stores. The bowl in a 6-litre gravity-type toilet is designed to enhance the siphoning action, which makes it possible to use less water than earlier designs. A dual-flush toilet has two buttons instead of a single lever for flushing, which allows the user to choose the amount of water in the flush. For liquid waste, the 3-litre flush is enough, while the regular 6-litre flush is needed for solid waste. It's a great water-saving technology.

Toilet design has some options too. Most people still buy traditional two-piece toilets. The base is one piece and the tank is

We've come a long way in water-saving technology for toilets: from 20-litre flushes to today's 6-litre standard.

I don't know how many times I've seen a heat register too close to a toilet. It's not good, for obvious reasons. Move your register or explore other heating sources like radiant heat.

the second. One-piece toilets are usually more expensive and better looking: it's just a sleeker design than a two-piece. That, and the fact that they are easier to clean (no crevice between the two pieces to get dirty), probably account for how popular one-piece toilets are becoming.

Prices range from $100 to several thousand dollars. But a high price doesn't necessarily mean better water savings or improved performance. Buy quality, but don't be taken in by all the flashy extras. Look for that wide throat opening, get the design that suits your tastes, and make sure that you have a seat before you buy to see if the height and shape of the bowl work for you.

Bathtubs

As with all the elements in your home, think about how you use a tub before you make your choice. If you prefer a shower and use the tub only for the kids, then choose a standard tub without any fanfare. But if you enjoy long baths, you may want to consider a specialized bathtub, such as a large soaker tub or a whirlpool with jets, and

Make sure your contractor knows early on which side of your bathtub you want the fixtures to be installed.

MIKE'S TIP

The right way to install a recessed bathtub

Any alcove or recessed tub has to be built in, which can be more challenging than it sounds.

A standard tub is said to be 5 feet long, but really it's a bit shorter so it'll fit into a 5-foot opening. At the top of almost any recessed tub is a lip, which acts as a drip barrier. Water that splashes against it should just flow back into the tub. A common mistake among contractors is to take the cement board that they're using for the walls (as a backer for tiles) and bring it right down to the tub. Because the lip doesn't actually sit tight against the wall (remember, the tub isn't quite 5 feet), bringing the cement board right down to the tub means bringing it in slightly at the bottom. You'll get non-square corners this way, which will be revealed in your tiles.

The better way is to have your contractor bring the cement board to the top of the lip, fill that 1-inch gap with thinset, and then bring the Kerdi membrane down to the tub. You'll have a cleaner, neater tile installation, and everything will be true, level, square, and watertight.

maybe even something large enough for two people. It's up to you, but choose carefully because this isn't something you can easily change later.

Tub styles

Alcove or recessed bathtubs are probably the most common style you'll see. These tubs have only one finished wall, because only that one faces out into the bathroom. A corner tub is triangular and also usually has only one of its sides finished because the other two are against walls, which makes it a lot like the alcove bathtub. Before you buy a recessed tub of any kind, make sure you know which side the plumbing is going on, since the tub will have the drain and overflow either on the right or left.

Drop-in tubs are supported on all sides by a frame, and they're "dropped into" an opening in the frame just like a drop-in sink is installed in the opening of a countertop. The tub is often built into a raised platform, but it can also be set below floor level, which gives a dramatic effect. Many drop-in tubs are made of lightweight acrylic, which makes it possible for them to be deeper and larger than a tub made from heavier material. Some have moulded seats for more comfort. Just like a drop-in sink, a drop-in bathtub needs to have that outer lip well sealed with silicone caulking at the point where the tub meets the platform.

Old claw-foot tubs are made of cast iron, so they can be very heavy. Newer acrylic tubs have the look of the old tubs with much less weight.

A freestanding tub stands alone, sometimes on feet (like the old-fashioned but still popular claw foot tub) and sometimes on a base. Freestanding tubs often have exposed pipes, so they're easier to install and service than built-in tubs, but the plumbing is visible, so it should be chrome—definitely an upgrade that will cost you extra, so make sure you find out exact costs and budget for it. If you're thinking of putting a freestanding tub in a central part of the bathroom, especially in a place where the bathtub has never sat before, make sure the structure is beefed up enough to support the load.

Tub materials

Bathtubs are manufactured in a range of materials, each with its own looks and benefits. I always recommend going for the heavier, more expensive end of the range, because you'll get better, longer-lasting quality that way.

Steel bathtubs coated with porcelain, usually referred to as porcelain bathtubs or POS (porcelain on steel), are the most common tubs sold. They're relatively inexpensive, lightweight, and durable, being fairly resistant to scratching and

Tempered glass is safer than regular glass for shower doors and walls.

chemicals. One drawback is their tendency to rust if the porcelain gets chipped or cracked.

Bathtubs made with traditional enamel on cast iron have been popular since they first appeared in the 1800s. Among the most expensive—and heaviest—tubs sold, they're also very durable, extremely resistant to chipping and scratching, and should last indefinitely with proper care. The look can be old-fashioned or not, and they now come in a range of different colours.

Fibreglass bathtubs are the least expensive tubs sold. They're light and fairly durable, though their colour will fade faster than many other materials.

Acrylic tubs have a glossy, attractive look. They're fairly sturdy and durable, but cost less than tubs made with a metal base. Acrylic is a popular choice for whirlpool baths and soaking tubs, because the lighter material compensates for the larger size and overall weight of the filled tub. Acrylic can be scratched by cleansers.

Solid stainless steel bathtubs are durable and easy to clean, but show water spots and minerals left behind by hard water. They're dramatic-looking, and are usually found in modern bathrooms that have other stainless steel fixtures or in bathrooms decorated in an industrial style.

Another new material for tubs, solid-surface material, has been available for years as a countertop material. It has excellent thermal properties and will keep bath water hot for longer than most other materials. And, just like when you use it on a countertop, you'll get real durability and good looks from solid surfacing.

Showers

Separate showers are getting to be a common feature in bathroom renovations. If you're tiling the area around the shower, do the same as you would with a tub and shower combination—cement board instead of drywall, with a waterproof membrane. For the bottom of the shower, I like the shower drain kits that are waterproof and sloped properly for drainage. The tile and threshold are installed on top of the kit.

Glass doors or walls in a shower should always be tempered glass for safety. Used in car windows too, tempered glass is manufactured so that if it breaks it shatters into small pieces instead of sharp pieces.

Countertops and backsplashes

When you're choosing a bathroom countertop, you have some of the same considerations as you do when you choose your kitchen countertop. The number one issue is how water-resistant the material is. But bathroom surfaces don't tend to take the beating that surfaces in the kitchen do, so durability is somewhat less of a concern. Remember that, just like with kitchen countertops, with bathroom counters you'll also have a choice of different nosing profiles to choose from. You'll want something that suits your overall design.

The backsplash in a bathroom, if you decide to use one, is often the same as the countertop, or else it's tile or tempered glass.

Granite

Granite is the most durable and easiest to care for of any of the natural stone materials. It's relatively expensive, but it's one of the most impressive-looking surfaces. You can save money by comparing prices at local stone shops, and should consider using leftovers from another homeowner's project if you don't need an especially large piece. Granite tiles are also more affordable than a single slab, and you can minimize the look of the grout lines by using a grout colour that blends with the granite rather than contrasting. Granite countertops need to be sealed every six months to a year. Stay away from abrasive cleaners as they'll scratch and dull the finish. Small chips and scratches can be polished down.

Manufactured quartz

Manufactured quartz imitates the look of limestone, granite, or marble, but is even more resistant to scratches and stains. Made up of 90% quartz particles, it comes in a variety of colours and thicknesses. In fact, four companies—Silestone, Okite, CaesarStone and DuPont's Zodiaq—make more than 130 styles of manufactured quartz countertops. Quartz is durable, easy to clean, and doesn't require sealing, making it a practical choice for the bathroom.

Solid-surface materials

Designed to look like natural stone, solid surface is one of the most popular counter-top options available. Usually referred to by brand names—Corian is probably the best known, but there's also Staron, Gibraltar, and Avonite—this easy-to-maintain synthetic product can be moulded to fit any design specification. The surface is non-porous and hypoallergenic, which is great in bathrooms, where mould and mildew are always concerns.

Composite marble

Composite marble is made from marble and a polyester resin and used to be available only in a glossy finish. Today, a matte finish that mimics the look of solid surface is also available. It lacks the durability of solid surface, so I don't recommend it when you're doing a renovation that should last a lifetime.

Concrete

You can fully customize your sink and countertop with concrete because you have the option to add coloured pigments, shape the edge any which way, and add creative inlays. But it's not water-resistant, especially as tiny cracks appear in the surface over time, and it can stain fairly easily. To keep a concrete countertop looking its best, it's advisable to seal it two to four times per year and wax with a paste every two to three months.

Wood

We're seeing more of these countertops in combination with furniture-type vanities, but water can cause a lot of damage to wood. If you really want to use wood, keep it for a low-use bathroom like a powder room, and make sure you've got many layers of a high-quality protective coating. Choosing a wood that's moisture-resistant—such as teak, afrormosia, or bilinga—will also help. Unfortunately, many of those unusually water-resistant woods are also exotic species of wood that we should be really reluctant to use.

Laminate

As in the kitchen, laminate is the most affordable countertop material on the market and comes in an array of colours and designs. Though it's maintenance-free, it can be scorched by curling irons and other hot appliances. Damaged areas can't be easily repaired.

Ceramic tile

This is an affordable option, and the style and finishes on porcelain and ceramic tile are almost limitless. Tiles are durable and water-resistant but the grout isn't. However, I don't recommend that you seal grout (ever) since it stops the grout from breathing and drying out properly. Instead, use a darker grout that will hide dirt better than pure white, or use less grout by going with larger tiles or tightening the grout lines. The best option of all is to use ceramic tile only on your floors and walls, and find a better countertop material.

The bathroom floor

There are three issues to think about when choosing a new bathroom floor: durability, moisture, and safety. Bathrooms get a lot of use and there's a lot of water flowing, even when you aren't running the shower, so you don't want to use materials that aren't going to stand up—or will let you slip up.

Bathroom countertops at a glance

Material	Granite, slate, marble	Solid-surface materials (such as Corian)	Plastic laminates (such as Arborite)	Quartz composite
Water-resistance	Low—must be sealed frequently	High	High	High
Cost	High	High	Low	Moderate to high
Environmental concerns	Uses natural but non-renewable resources	Manufacturing process is not environmentally friendly	Manufacturing process is not environmentally friendly	Manufacturing process is not environmentally friendly, though some natural and recycled materials are used
Good to know	Once seal has worn off, these are among the most porous surfaces, but they can be resealed	Available in almost any colour and profile	Must be well-sealed around faucets and sinks to prevent water damage to particleboard core	One of the most durable and non-porous countertops available
Recommended by Mike	Yes, if maintained	Yes	Yes	Yes

You can use almost any material you want for the floor, including wood, but you have to decide how much work you want to do on a daily basis to maintain it, and also consider the long-term damage that moisture can do to some materials. I don't think carpet is a good idea in the bathroom, even though there are carpet tiles on the market that can be removed and cleaned and put down again and again. I don't think most people want to do the upkeep and I don't recommend this option. Trust me, I've seen actual mushrooms growing in bathroom carpets because the carpets never dried out properly.

Wood is another "iffy" option. If you want to install a wood floor because you've got an older home and you want to match the period style, there are some extra things you're going to have to do. Use wood putty in the cracks so moisture won't seep between or under the boards, apply several extra coats of an oil-based polyurethane top coat, dry the water off the floor after every shower or bath, and make sure your contractor installs a highly efficient ventilation fan in the bathroom to help keep humidity to a minimum. Is a wood floor my first choice? No. Do I recommend it? No.

If you want a "warm" option for the bathroom floor without the maintenance hassle of wood, bamboo and cork each offer unique properties that can make them good choices for bathrooms. Bamboo floors look similar to traditional wood floors, but are naturally harder and more durable. Cork offers a soft, warm feel on bare feet. Both cork and bamboo are naturally resistant to mould, mildew, and bacteria, and

Composite marble	Concrete	Wood	Stainless steel	Tempered glass	Ceramic tiles
High	Low—must be sealed frequently	Low	High	High	High, but grout's is low
Moderate	High	Moderate to high	High	Moderate to high	Moderate
Uses some natural but non-renewable resources	Uses natural and renewable resources	Uses natural and renewable resources	Manufacturing process is not environmentally friendly	Manufacturing process is not environmentally friendly	Uses renewable resources and some recycled materials
Available in dozens of colours and glossy or matte finish	Requires sealing two to four times a year and waxing every three months	Best in low-use bathroom like powder room	Easily scratched; does not stain but does show fingerprints	Vulnerable to blows on exposed edges	Use darker grout to conceal dirt, or larger tiles for less grout
Yes	No	No	No	Yes	No

MIKE'S TIP

Protect your natural stone tiles.

Natural stone is a great product to use on bathroom floors, but there are issues you should know about.

First, natural stone needs to be sealed. The ideal time to do this is when the tile has been installed, but before the grout goes on. When the thinset under the tiles is dry, a high-quality sealer (something that will penetrate the stone, not just sit on top) should be rolled on. Two coats of sealer is best. Some of these products are called "sealer enhancers" and they really do bring out the beauty of the stone. I recommend a matte finish rather than gloss because I think the gloss shows the defects in the stone, whereas the matte finish always looks great.

If you're using a light-coloured marble tile, you have something else to think about. The standard type of thinset comes in a dark grey colour. That's usually not a problem because you never see it: it gets trowelled onto the floor or wall and the tiles cover it up. But with a light-coloured marble, dark thinset can cause discolouration over time. The marble will absorb some of the colour, and you'll see a gradual darkening that you probably won't like.

The solution is to get your installer to use a white-based polymer thinset. It's much lighter in colour, and your marble tiles will keep their pure white look.

When you consider how much you pay for every square foot of natural stone tile, it's worth taking these extra steps.

both naturally repel moisture, which of course are excellent qualities in bathroom floors. And both are environmentally sound choices because they're both sustainable and renewable resources.

Vinyl is the most popular choice for bathroom floors because there are thousands of options, and it's inexpensive and very easy to maintain. But there are a lot of drawbacks. For one, the mastic (usually it's a glue) used to fix the flooring to the subfloor is very prone to mould—and there's no better place for mould to grow than in a wet bathroom. You should also think hard about the fact that vinyl fails the environmentally friendly test both in production and in the effects the new floor will have on your indoor air quality for some time after it's installed.

Stone—whether it's marble, granite, limestone, slate, or any other stone—is a relatively good choice because there are no moisture problems as long as the stone is sealed before installation, and sealed again every couple of years. The drawback is that all these stone floors are cold, and they're slippery. There are solutions, though.

Tiles can be installed on the floor and walls.

In-floor heating can make them feel great underfoot. And you can have the stone tiles sandblasted or purchase naturally textured stone, such as slate, to minimize slipping. The other drawback? Any type of stone is by far your most expensive flooring option.

The colour in porcelain tiles is the same throughout the tile so the colour can't chip off like it can with ceramic tiles.

In my opinion the best choice for the bathroom floor is ceramic or porcelain tile. Like stone, these have a rich, textured, solid feeling. They're waterproof and fairly affordable. And like wood flooring, they look really good. There are so many different types of ceramic tiles, you can get exactly the floor you want. You can even find ceramic tile that looks like stone, or wood. It comes in many sizes, and in a variety of shapes such as octagonal and hexagonal. Mosaic tiles come in pre-mounted plastic mesh sheets, so each tile doesn't need to be set individually. With tinted grout, you can be even more creative. Tile cleans up well and resists even standing pools of water. Downsides: Like stone, it's cold. Also, it can be slippery. But textured tiles solve that problem. Smaller tiles are less slippery, because more grout is used and the grout acts as a non-skid surface. Just make sure you don't seal the grout, because it needs to breathe.

With any type of tile you choose for walls and floors, proper installation is critical, of course. Schluter makes a great product that's called Ditra. A light coat of thinset is installed first, followed by the Ditra (dimpled plastic material that rolls out like a sheet), then another layer of thinset, and then the tiles over that. It provides a cushion that prevents tile cracking and keeps any moisture from getting through to the flooring and framing below the tile layer.

Mike's picks for bathroom upgrades

You may be limited by size and budget, but there are lots of upgrade options that can turn one of the smallest rooms in your house into one of your favourite spots.

In-floor heat

One of the ultimate luxuries is warmth underfoot. In-floor heat can be installed under many different types of flooring, but ceramic, porcelain, and marble are ideal for heated floors since they hold the heat so well. Although thicker floors made of stone take longer to transfer heat, they'll also retain warmth for a longer time. The easiest way to get radiant in-floor heat is with a heat mat such as Nuheat. It's an electrical coil sewn into a fibreglass fabric. Your electrician will install it along with a programmable thermostat before the finish layer of flooring goes in.

Towel warmers

The same warming drawers that can be found in the kitchen are beginning to show up in the bathroom, installed in the vanity. If you put your towels in before your bath or shower, they'll be warm by the time you're ready for them. Another option is a heated towel rack or towel bar, which can be free standing or wall mounted. Heated towel racks and bars do double duty warming up your towels before use and drying them quickly afterward to keep them fresher longer. This is a luxury upgrade that's quite inexpensive. It should be hard-wired by your electrician, so make sure this is part of your plans from the start.

Bathroom floors at a glance

Material	Ceramic or porcelain tile	Natural stone, slate, limestone, or marble tile	Linoleum	Vinyl	Cork
Durability	Extremely high	Extremely high	Very high	Depends on grade	Fairly high
Water-resistance	High	High	High	High	High
Range of colours/ patterns	Almost unlimited	Limited to natural colours	Many colours, but limited patterns	Broad	Broad range of stain colours; patterns can be created
Cost	Moderate to high	Moderate to high	Moderate	Low to moderate	Moderate to high
Environmental concerns	Uses renewable resources; energy requirements to produce ceramic tile are high	Uses natural but non-renewable products; may be transported over long distances	Uses non-toxic, renewable resources; biodegradable	Manufacturing process is not environmentally friendly; will off-gas in the home	Uses bark rather than whole trees; may be transported over long distances
Good to know	Can be cold and slippery when wet	Can be cold and slippery when wet	Resists bacteria, but adhesive used is not mould-resistant	Mastics are prone to mould	Naturally repels water and insects; must be sealed
Recommended by Mike for bathroom use?	Yes	Yes	No	No	Yes

Soaker tub

The noisy Jacuzzi tub has been replaced by the free-standing, luxurious soaker tub. Add massaging features with air jets that massage you all over or can be programmed to hit strategic areas.

Tankless water heater

To make your bathroom function well from the inside out, replace your hot water heater with a tankless (on-demand) water heater. With no tank there's no standby heat loss. You'll get up to 40% higher efficiency and up to 80% lower nitrogen oxide emissions than with a standard hot water tank.

Hardwood	Glass tile	Laminates ("click" flooring)	Bamboo	Carpet
Fairly high	Extremely high	Moderate	Fairly high	Depends on grade
Moderate	High	Moderate	Moderate	Low
Broad range of stain colours; patterns can be created	Almost unlimited	Broad	Broad range of stain colours; patterns can be created	Broad range of colours only
Moderate to high	Moderate to high	Low to moderate	Moderate to high	Low to moderate
Uses natural and renewable resources (FSC rating)	Recycled glass tile is easily available	Manufacturing process is not environmentally friendly	Uses a fast-growing, renewable resource; may be transported over long distances	Manufacturing process is not environmentally friendly; carpet will off-gas in first months after installation
Can be dented and scratched by normal use	Can be slippery when wet unless you use a rough finish	Warranty may be void if used in wet areas	Installs much like hardwood	Hard to keep clean in wet areas
No	Yes	No	Yes	No

Following up: Checklist

Now's the time to make and record your choices for your bathroom reno. Use the following checklist to keep track of your decisions.

Layout

Basic layout (attach drawing) _____

Checked against design "rules" for efficient design and operation?_____

Cabinetry

Custom or stock?_____

Material and finish: _____

Product name/number (if applicable):_____

Special features: _____

Lighting
(show placement of all light fixtures on drawing)

Type and number of fixtures for general lighting: _____

Product name/number:_____

Type and number of fixtures for task lighting: _____

Product name/number:_____

Type and number of fixtures for accent lighting: _____

Product name/number:_____

Other electrical needs

Number of GFCI outlets (show placement on drawing):_____

Other wiring needed for telephone, cable, Internet access: _____

Type of ceiling fan/light combination:_____

Product name/number of ceiling fan/light: _____

Light and fan on same switch, or separate?_____

Electric towel warmers?_____

Heat lamps? _____

Whirlpool tub that requires electrical power? _____

Electrical in-floor heat?_____

Plumbing fixtures

Type of sink, and number of holes needed for faucet: _____

Product name/number of sink: _____

Product name/number of faucet: _____

Type of bathtub: _____

Plumbing on left or right side of bathtub, or free standing? _____

Product name/number of bathtub: _____

Product name/number of faucet: _____

Separate shower or combined with bath? _____

Product name/number of faucet and shower head: _____

Extra shower heads or nozzles? _____

Countertops and backsplash

Type of countertop: _____

Total square footage: _____

Nosing profile: _____

Product name/number/colour: _____

Backsplash type (if different from countertop): _____

Product name/number/colour of backsplash: _____

Flooring

Type of flooring: _____

Total square footage: _____

Product name/number/colour: _____

CHAPTER 7

Built to Last

Years and years ago, skilled trades built our country, they built the homes and the churches, and many of these are still standing today. But the crap that we're building now isn't going to last a decade. Not without costing you a lot of money, because we don't care anymore. It's no longer about craftsmanship. It's all about money.

I want to get rid of building without caring, and building without knowing why we do things, not just how. With the Holmes Foundation, I'm working to help train the next generation of skilled trades so they build it right. That means doing it better. Professionals keep their minds open to different techniques and different products because not only does it make their world easier, it makes your world better too.

If we think more about building for longevity, then we're building smart. We should be building homes with a better lumber that's going to last longer, with a better drywall that's not going to mould, and continue to build from the outside in and not the inside out. We can start thinking about fireproof houses, mould-free houses, watertight and truly green homes. Should we be doing this? Should we demand this? Well, let me ask you, why not? Do you really want something that's built to minimum code? The answer's no. We need to do better.

If we can introduce all the right products in our renovations, we'll spend our money right the first time and never have to do it again. I see houses that have bathrooms that are 60 years old and they look outdated, but they're still in good shape. In one home, a wonderful old lady loved to clean and she took care of her bathroom. And 60 years later that bathroom was perfect.

Your house doesn't come with a manual, like a refrigerator, like your stereo system. And your house doesn't have a maintenance schedule like a car, but you're not off the hook. Take care of your renovation and your house. If you have counters or floors that need to be sealed regularly, keep it up. Look under your sink for water damage, keep your house clean and check your drains regularly. And every year do a thorough inspection of the outside of your house, including looking at the caulking of your windows, your eavestroughs, and your roof.

The perfect kitchen or bathroom of your dreams, with the right products, installed right, will last many years. And by paying attention to what's underneath your renovation, such as structure, plumbing, and electrical, down the road if you want to update your room or add new features, any future changes will be much easier. Do it right and take care and your house should outlast you.

Kitchen or bath renovation: Step-by-step checklist

Every renovation is different, but the preparation process is pretty much the same.

STEP ONE: Planning (one to three months)

- ❏ **Start an ideas file. Buy a few folders to keep magazine clippings, pamphlets, product flyers, copies of your contract, any change orders that come up, etc.**
- ❏ **Take "before" photographs, and continue to photograph the job at every stage. Photos are helpful in the event of disputes, and for later reference.**
- ❏ **Consult a kitchen or bathroom designer, or use your own design, to do preliminary plan drawings and basic product and material specifications.**
- ❏ **Assess the existing space. Consult a general contractor or a specialized contractor (plumber, electrician, etc.), or hire a home inspector to thoroughly inspect your house. A home inspection can help identify potential problems and may even show that your money is better spent somewhere else, such as a leaky roof.**
- ❏ **Always check and test for environmental hazards like asbestos and lead before you start.**
- ❏ **Using the assessments above, decide on your renovation priorities and determine your budget. Make sure financing is in place.**

STEP TWO: Hiring your contractor

- ❏ **Begin the process of hiring a general contractor. Investigate at least six candidates using the same interview questions for each. Ask for referrals and follow up with phone calls and visits to previous projects. Make sure each candidate visits your house in person. Submit copies of your plan drawings and basic material and product specifications to each contractor for written bids.**
- ❏ **Compare bids, qualifications (including licensing and insurance), and the results of referral checks for each contractor. Hire one contractor.**
- ❏ **Together with the contractor, finalize your construction and design plans, including drawings and material specifications.**

Create a detailed contract that specifies the scope and cost of the project. Complete material and product specifications, a work and payment schedule, and a contingency process ("extras").

❏ Make your first payment to the contractor, never more than 10% of the total cost of the job.

❏ Determine who will seek building permits (you or the contractor). Keep permits and inspection reports in a file folder at the job site for referral at any time. Post the permit notice in your window.

❏ Order any custom or special-order products, such as windows, countertops, and cabinets.

❏ Notify your insurer about the scope and timeline of your renovation and ensure that you are covered for the project.

STEP THREE: Demolition and construction

❏ Prepare the space by removing furniture and personal belongings.

❏ Have the contractor seal off the construction zone with plastic sheeting.

❏ Begin demolition. Reuse or recycle where possible. Contact Habitat for Humanity to ask if they may be able to use some of your materials.

❏ Do any necessary structural repairs or reinforcements (with permits followed by inspections).

❏ Frame walls and doors.

❏ Install windows.

❏ Rough in the electrical circuits, plumbing, and duct work, followed by inspections.

❏ Insulate with closed-cell polyurethane foam insulation (or batt insulation and separate vapour barrier), followed by inspection.

❏ Install the subfloor (and in-floor heat, if using).

❏ Install drywall: tape, mud, and sand.

❏ Paint: primer and two finish coats.

❏ Install finish flooring.

❏ Install cabinetry, countertops, and trim.

❏ Install plumbing fixtures, followed by plumbing inspection.

❏ Install electrical outlets and lighting fixtures, followed by electrical inspection.

❏ Install other finishing touches.

STEP FOUR: Completion (six weeks)

❏ Do final walk-through with the contractor. Make a list of touch-ups needed, and monitor progress until all touch-ups are completed.

❏ Make payment due on "substantial completion." Hold back 10% until 45 days have passed and you have received proof that all subtrades and suppliers have been paid.

Glossary

ABS (Acrylonitrile Butadiene Styrenesome). Hard black plastic plumbing pipes, used primarily for drainage. The rule of thumb for drainage pipes is ABS pipes in your house and PVC for in-ground pipes. Some municipalities forbid the use of ABS pipe for any application.

AFCI (arc fault circuit interrupter). An electrical device in your circuit panel that cuts power to prevent electrical fires when the AFCI detects minute differences in electrical current caused by punctured wires, shorts, and arcing. *See also* GFCI.

Amperes (or amps). An electrical unit of measurement that tells the rate of electrical charge flowing through the system. Electrical service panels and circuit breakers are usually measured in amps.

Arc. A short circuit where the electricity literally jumps, or arcs, to the nearest metal.

Backsplash. The wall between the top of a kitchen counter and the bottom of cabinets. Backsplashes, especially behind the kitchen sink, are susceptible to splashing water and must therefore be made of, or covered by, a waterproof or water-resistant material.

Batt. Fibreglass, mineral wool, and cotton insulation are usually sold in rectangular batts, a fluffy material (much like cotton candy). In walls, insulation batts are placed between studs.

Bay. The space between the rafters in an attic.

Beam. A wooden or steel member that runs horizontally in the opposite direction to the joists, helping to support the structure above.

Building code. The building code sets out the minimum standards for framing and foundations that will ensure that a house is going to be safe and secure. The code is fairly uniform across North America, though there are special provisions in some regions to protect against local dangers, such as earthquakes or hurricanes. Separate codes deal with a house's plumbing and electrical systems.

Building inspector. A municipal employee who inspects a home as it's being built or renovated to ensure that the work meets the minimum local building code.

Caulk/caulking. Flexible sealant that is used to stop air or water penetration. Caulk comes in many strengths and varieties. The most common caulks are made from latex and silicone.

Cement board. A harder, heavier, and more waterproof alternative to drywall, made from cement sandwiched between two layers of fiberglass mesh. Cement board is advisable for areas with heavy moisture since it will not mould like regular drywall.

Centres. The distance between the middle of two studs (or joists). For example, in modern houses, the distance from the centre of one stud to the centre of the next is usually 16¾", often spoken of as "16 inches on centre," or written as "16" o.c." This distance ensures adequate structural support, and the standard measurement allows for drywall or other coverings to be easily attached to the studs.

Cinder block. Often used in foundations, cinder blocks are made of concrete and coal cinders.

Circuit. Electricity flows in a circuit, from the service panel to various outlets and fixtures and then back to the panel. Each circuit is rated for amps, which are controlled by a circuit breaker, commonly 15 or 20 amps. A circuit controlled by a 20-amp breaker is capable of safely carrying 1,800 watts (20 amps x 120 volts x 80% for safety). Ten outlets is usually the maximum for a circuit (fewer if those outlets are serving appliances that draw a lot of electricity, such as window air conditioners).

Circuit breaker. A protective device in an electrical panel that interrupts the flow of electricity in an electrical circuit when there is an excess load or a short. Older service panels used fuses, but they were replaced by circuit breakers, which are easier to reset.

Cold zone. An area within a house that isn't heated, such as an attic or crawl space. It's critical that cold zones have proper ventilation to avoid moisture buildup and rot.

Concrete. A construction material made from a mixture of cement, sand, stone, and water. There are many different types of concrete available, and it's critical to use the right one for the right job and not to allow concrete to harden too quickly.

Crawl space. A shallow, unfinished space beneath the first floor of a building. Crawl spaces are sometimes built instead of full-height basements.

Crown. The natural bow in a piece of wood, a visible curve. It's critical when framing a house that all the crowns face the same direction. In a vertical wall, the crowns should face out; on the floor, the crowns should face up.

Ditra. A brand-name product from Schluter, Ditra is a waffled orange plastic material that is used under tiles to help prevent them from cracking.

Drywall. The most common interior wall material, drywall is made from gypsum (a chalk-like mineral) sandwiched between two layers of heavy paper. Drywall comes in many different types and thicknesses, including denser drywalls for ceilings, fire-rated drywalls, and water-resistant and mould-proof drywalls for high-moisture areas.

Drywall compound. Often called "mud," drywall compound is a paste that is used to fill and cover the seams in drywall sheets.

Ducts. The round or rectangular sheet metal pipes in which air flows from a forced air furnace. The main duct from the furnace is called the plenum, and individual ducts run off the plenum to rooms throughout the house.

Efflorescence. A white, salty crystal-like deposit commonly seen on foundation walls. The presence of efflorescence is a sign of water invasion in basements.

Engineered wood. Hardwood flooring that is made of three to five layers of wood stacked and bonded together under heat and pressure.

Fascia. A long, flat board fastened to the ends of the eaves on roofing rafters. This is on the exterior of the house.

Feed lines. Plumbing pipes in which water is supplied to the house or to an individual fixture (such as a sink or bathtub). Modern feed lines are usually copper or Pex tubing.

Fisheye. Small (but undesirable) air bubbles that may show up in drywall compound as it's applied.

Flashing. The thin sheet metal around the chimney, dormers, skylights, and so forth. In the case of the chimney, for example, the flashing rests flush against the chimney and then goes under the shingles.

Footings. Foundation walls rest on concrete footings, which in turn rest on undisturbed earth. Footings should be twice the width of the wall itself.

Forced air. A common form of heating, featuring a powerful fan that forces warm air throughout the house via ducts in the walls. Forced air furnaces can be powered by natural gas, electricity, propane, or oil.

Foundation. The foundation bears the weight of the house and holds up against the pressure of the earth around it. Foundations can be made of a variety of materials including fieldstone, brick, concrete block, poured concrete, and insulated concrete forms. Foundations are usually dug at least four feet into the ground, below the frost line.

Geothermal system. A heating system that captures heat from deep in the ground. Geothermal systems may be used to supplement more traditional home heating methods.

GFCI (ground fault circuit interrupter). This protects people from severe electric shocks and electrocution. A GFCI monitors the amount of current flowing from hot to neutral circuits; if there is a difference—even as small as 4 or 5 milliamps, amounts too small to activate a fuse or circuit breaker—it cuts the electricity in a fraction of a second. *See also* AFCI.

Grout. A thin mortar for filling joints between tiles. Grout can be cement-based or epoxy.

HRV (heat recovery ventilation unit). An HRV brings fresh air into the furnace and exhausts stale air. A heat exchanger in the HRV recovers heat from the outgoing air and preheats incoming air to help reduce energy costs.

Header. In a wooden stud wall, the 2 x 4 above the window or door is called a header.

Home inspector. A person who, independently or in association with a small or nationwide home inspection company, inspects homes to assist potential buyers in making real estate decisions. Services usually include the inspection and a written report, and are charged on either a flat-rate or an hourly basis.

House wrap. A house wrap sheds moisture from the outside even while it allows air to flow through its microscopic holes. The air movement allows moisture to move back through to the outside. The most popular house wrap brands are Tyvek and Typar.

HVAC. An acronym for the heating, ventilation, and air conditioning systems in a house.

Jack stud. A second vertical stud used to reinforce the structure of a stud frame wall where a door will be installed.

Joists. Horizontal, parallel beams, usually placed on their edge to support the floors and walls in a house.

Junction box. A metal box where separate lines are run off the circuit to receptacles and lights.

Kerdi. A brand-name product from Schluter, Kerdi is a membrane that can be used on floors and walls to create a waterproof barrier before installing stone, ceramic, or porcelain tiles.

Knob and tube. The oldest form of electrical wiring, installed until about 1945. The system featured two separate wires, one black and one white, for each circuit, unlike today's electrical wires, which combine black, white, and ground wires. Knob and tube refers to the ceramic knobs the wire was strung from and the tubes used to protect the wire where it passed through joists and studs.

Laminate floor. A flooring system comprised of interlocking panels. Each panel is made up of an inner core of pressed and glued wood material, with a photographic image of wood laminated on the surface.

Lath. Before drywall became the common choice for interior walls, small slats of wood (lath) were nailed horizontally to the wall studs with a narrow gap between each piece of lath. Thick layers of plaster were then applied to the lath to make a smooth covering.

Lien. A legal claim made by one person on another person's property as security on a debt. A contractor (or subcontractor) may place a lien on a house when they have not been paid so that if the house is sold they are repaid from the proceeds.

Load-bearing wall. A wall that is integral to the construction of the house. It cannot be safely removed without building new supports (various solutions are possible) that will bear an equal load.

Mastic. A cement adhesive used to fix tiles to floors, specifically vinyl and linoleum.

MDF (medium density fibreboard). Because it doesn't have the structural strength of solid wood or plywood, MDF is not recommended in many applications, but MDF crown moulding and trim are popular, lower-cost options.

Mould. A fungus that grows on organic materials such as wood or paper, especially when moisture is present.

Mud. *See* drywall compound.

Non-vitreous. *See* porosity.

Off-gassing. Off-gassing happens when chemicals are released into the air by a non-metallic substance, such as paint, varnish, or glue. Known as volatile organic compounds (VOCs), the chemicals in off-gases have a wide range of impacts from relatively mild—stinging eyes, irritated nasal passages, and nausea—to potentially life-threatening.

OSB (oriented strand board). A modern version of plywood that uses layers of wood flakes, fibres, or strands bonded together under intense heat and pressure. The direction of the fibres is alternated between layers for greater strength.

Pex. A plumbing system that uses flexible plumbing tubes made from aluminum sandwiched between two layers of heat-resistant polyethylene.

Plaster. Common in homes built before the 1940s, plaster is made from gypsum mixed with water and fibrous material. Horsehair was sometimes added to strengthen the plaster before it was applied over wooden lath in plaster-and-lath walls.

Plenum. *See* ducts.

PVC (polyvinyl chloride). Plastic used in plumbing pipes (usually white or grey). When it is used as a drainage pipe, PVC connects to the city sewer system or a septic system. When it comes to drain pipes, the standard rule is ABS for the vent stack and PVC for the in-ground drainage.

Porosity. The ability of a material to absorb water. For stone and tile, porosity is graded using the following system: the least absorbent is called "impervious," followed by "vitreous," "semi-vitreous," and finally, the most porous, "non-vitreous."

R-value. The R-value of any material—usually insulation—measures how well that material resists the loss of heat if the temperature on one side of it is higher than on the other side. Basically, the higher the R-value, the better the material insulates.

Rigid foam. Not to be confused with white Styrofoam, rigid foam is made from either extruded polystyrene (often seen as pink and blue boards) or expanded polyisocyanurate. Rigid foam is commonly used for insulating foundations and as a thermal and vapour break in basements.

Rough in. In plumbing and electrical work, "rough in" is the stage when an inspection by a building or electrical inspector should occur. The pipes or wires have been installed, but the walls and floors have not been closed in and the fixtures have not been connected.

Service panel. All electricity entering a house first goes into a service panel, a wall-mounted box, usually in the basement, which features breakers for individual circuits.

Stud. One of a series of wood or metal vertical structures in walls and partitions. Wood studs are usually 2 x 4s, though 2 x 6s are also used, especially for exterior walls, to allow for adequate insulation.

Subfloor. Attached to the supporting joists underneath it, the subfloor is as it sounds: what is below your floor covering. In older houses, the subfloor was often broad planks; in newer houses, it is usually OSB or plywood.

Thermal barrier. A material (such as plastic) used between warm areas (such as the interior of a house) and cold areas (such as the exterior, in northern climates in winter) to lessen moisture buildup and heat loss.

Thermal break. A material (such as foam) that completely separates warm areas (such as the interior of a house) from cold areas (such as the exterior, in northern climates in winter). Because cold and hot do not meet at all, there is no moisture buildup or heat loss. The best analogy is a beverage cooler: the built-in foam insulation acts as a thermal break to keep cold drinks completely separated from warm air outside.

Thinset. A mixture of cement, very finely graded sand, and additives that allow the cement to properly hydrate. "Modified" thinset has additional polymers added to improve adhesion—basically, thinset with more glue.

Truss. A prefabricated triangular roof support. Trusses come in a wide variety of sizes and shapes.

UFFI (urea formaldehyde foam insulation). This insulation contains high levels of formaldehyde. It off-gasses into the air and can cause health problems in humans. It was banned in Canada in 1980.

Vent stack. Also called "the stack" or the "waste and vent stack," the vent stack is a vertical pipe that carries water and waste down to the drainage pipe in the basement. Open at the top, and typically sticking out through the roof of your house, the stack also lets sewer gases escape and provides air for drains and toilets to empty properly.

VOCs (volatile organic compounds). The chemicals in off-gases that have a wide range of impacts from relatively mild—stinging eyes, irritated nasal passages, and nausea—to potentially life-threatening.

Vapour barrier. Usually a 6-mil polyethylene plastic sheet, vapour barrier is stapled to the studs on the warm side of an exterior wall (usually this means the interior side of the insulation) to prevent water vapour from getting into the studding.

Acknowledgements

Last year, I had the privilege of being a part of the World Skills Competition in Calgary, where the best professionals from around the world competed. Their passion, precision, and craftsmanship was inspiring and a sign of a whole new generation of trades workers who take pride in their work and care about what they do. I see the same passion in our work with The Holmes Foundation and in the recipients of our bursaries and scholarships. I'm grateful to everyone who supports our foundation and its mission to ensure that all residential renovation and construction in Canada is done right—the first time.

My passion for the trades was inspired by my dad and his commitment to always make it right. Every day I get to work with people who share that belief. I always say that you're only as good as the people who surround you, and I get to work with the best, including my kids, Amanda, Sherry, and Mike—every father should be so lucky. To everyone at The Holmes Group, my greatest appreciation.

This book would not be possible without the commitment and insight of Liza Drozdov, Pete Kettlewell, and Michael Quast. Special thanks to HarperCollins Canada, especially Brad Wilson, Noelle Zitzer, Alan Jones, and Neil Erickson for their expertise, dedication, and passion.

Finally, to all the contractors who care about making it right, thanks and keep doing what you do.

Index